God Loves You This Much!

A Story of Love, Loss, and Leaning Into Jesus

Susie Wirth

Dedication

Relevant girls, this book is dedicated to you! Although I may not be able to sit down with each of you and share stories over a cup of coffee, I want you to feel as if you really know me. I believe what God has taught me through the ups and downs in my life can be a help to those that have experienced hurt or loss in their lives. My prayer and hope is that each of you grow closer to our Lord as you read my stories and share with one another, for each of us are made to be loved and belong. May we each truly know, God Loves You This Much!

Contents

Introduction

In about 2003 a group of lovely, Godly ladies in our church approached me and asked me if I would join them in the prayer room so they could pray over me. All of the pastors' wives were also going to be prayed over. So, I went into the little prayer room at the church and they began to pray over each of the pastors' wives. It was a pretty large church so I remember there were about 10 of us in the room. When they finally came to me, one of the ladies kneeled down in front of me and began saying, "I see so much pain. I am just overwhelmed at the amount of suffering and pain." Then they all prayed over me and I felt really encouraged and uplifted in the Spirit. However, what I didn't realize at the time was she was basically prophesizing over me. As I contemplated that event in my life, I asked myself, "Am I giving off an aura of pain and suffering?" I mean, do I look like this? I know I have a special needs child and I know I have had my share of pain, but I don't want to be known as pain.

In a more direct way a few years later, a pastor friend of ours was sitting across a dining room table from Paul and me. He said, "You both will speak to thousands, but it will be through much pain."

It has only been recently I have remembered these two prophecies that were spoken over my life. Honestly, I have really tried to forget them because I don't like it. I didn't ask for it, and I don't want it. However, what I have come to understand is God is using my pain and my story, to help and heal those with hurting hearts. Additionally, I do not have to live under the cloak of pain, but I do have the choice every day to live in the fruit of the Spirit of love, joy, peace, gentleness, and goodness

One significant thing in my life that I have learned is our stories matter. We have an inner longing to have a witness to our lives. We desire someone to notice when we are sad and enter into our happiness when we are happy. Even if it is only one person, we feel loved. This is the human connection. We sense we belong in this world, and belonging brings value to our existence. Still, more than belonging and feeling loved, our stories matter because they teach. We will not all walk the same road, but we can learn to be better human beings when we have compassion for one another. We grow when we get our focus off our condition and see the needs of someone else. Finally, Revelations 12:11 tells us, "we overcome him by the blood of the lamb and the word of our testimony." Our story reflects our testimony which is what we believe about God, Jesus, the work of the Holy Spirit in our lives, and so much more. My story matters and your story matters. God uses every part of our stories. They make us who we are. I am just a regular girl, called by God to be the wife of a pastor, and a mom to two strong, beautiful children, one of whom is an adult with special needs. I am learning how to love, experience loss with grace, as I lean into Jesus, and this is the word of my testimony…my story.

1 MY SONG

In the spring of 2010, I found myself at a point of crisis in my faith journey. I was wrestling with many questions, not the least of which was, "Does God really love me?" I felt so desperate at times I secretly said to myself, "if this is His perfect plan for my life, then He must not love me very much." That conclusion was the only thing I could come up with for why I had been dealt so many seasons of loss and hurt in my life. So, my wrestling began. I would ask myself where in my journey had God made a mistake if indeed He had? Next, I would feel shameful for questioning God and ask myself to what degree does anyone have the right to question the Almighty. I really felt guilty questioning His love for me. After all, I am a Pastor's wife. I'm 49 years old. Shouldn't I have all the questions of life answered by now? As you can see, my turmoil was quite maddening. So how did I come to this point of questioning anyway? Let me back up and start somewhat from the beginning. I think you might be able to follow along a little better knowing my backstory.

As a young child, I was very much a daydreamer. I loved to pretend and almost every Saturday evening my sisters and I would make up choreographic dance routines to The Lawrence Welk Show while our mother lay on the couch in amusement by our dance. Music seemed to be a significant part of me as a young child. The songs sang in my childhood remain with me today. The influence of that music is part of what makes me who

I am. The influencers of my life were mostly those who sang for me and with me. I guess since music spoke to me, those who joined me in my love of music were some of the strongest influences of my life. My Grandmother shared my love of music, or I should say, I shared her love for music. I remember admiring my grandmother as she would play the piano and sing. She would play by ear and sing out in her strong alto voice. She always sang songs about Jesus and the old-time religion. One particular song she sang was about an old-time preacher man. Since my Daddy was a preacher, it was fun to hear her sing this song. I recall some of the words.

Old time preacher man, preachin bout the Promised land and not old worldly things.

Old time preacher man preachin bout the sins of man, preached it mighty plain.

Down at the altar rail oh how sinners fell, my how he proclaimed.

I believe our God's the same today as He was yesterday.

I can even hear a hymn today and Grandma's strong alto voice comes through my mind making the harmony rich and sweet.

Another musical influence in my young life was my Dad. Some of the sweetest and most vivid memories I have with my dad are lying on the floor next to our old stereo. It was so big it almost took up the length of an entire wall. I would curl up next to my daddy and he would put his arm around me and we would just listen and sing along to Gospel music together. Since my dad had to prepare his Sunday messages each week as part of his meditation and preparation, this private worship time was a regular occurrence. Except when I would make it not so private and come snuggle up next to him on the floor. So, at about age five, it was no wonder I had several songs memorized. Everyone thought it was so cute when I sang my first solo at church at five years old. I wish I had a picture because I am sure my mom put those white plastic knee-high boots from the early 70's on me for my first grand performance!

As I grew up my fondness for music grew even more. At about nine years old I started learning how to play the piano. It became my obsession. It was more of a love affair than a hobby for me. I was totally addicted to singing and playing the piano. My other siblings will attest to my addiction because at least once a day I would hear a door shut abruptly when I decided to sit down at the piano and have a Susie sing-along session. The only problem was it really was just a solo recital each time. I would spend hours at the piano singing and playing. I played several styles of music like romantic love songs, the standards, and most frequently, worship songs. My love for the Lord grew as I sang and worshiped on that brown upright piano in the living room. Regardless of what was going on in my family around me, I carried on in my own little dreamer's world. There was one song in particular that became a favorite of mine. It was really a song of tragedy and it was written out of the broken heart of a young woman who lost her husband early in their marriage. This song impacted me so much because of the true story behind it that it almost became my signature song. I would sing this song as solos and was even asked to perform it as a guest singer in other local churches.

Little did I know this song would not just be the signature song I would sing but would become the theme song I would live! This song was so powerful in my heart it was the trigger for what began my wrestling with God over this His love for me.

The lyrics are as follows
"My life I give to You Oh Lord.
Use me I pray.
May I glorify Your precious name
In all I do and say.

Let me trust You in the valley dark
As well as in the light,
Knowing You will always lead me;
Your will is always right.

I know God makes no mistakes.
He leads in every path I take
Along the way that's leading me to home.
Tho' at times my heart would break,
There's a purpose in every change He makes;
That others would see my life and know
That God makes no mistakes"[1]

I carried this song in my heart with me everywhere. Anytime a random solo was called for this song was my ole stand by. Right after college, my music world took a turn from being almost my all to almost nothing at all in my life. When I married, I didn't have a piano to play and sing, so I simply drifted away from my old habit. Being married consumed most of my down time and working in the real world consumed any energy I had left. It wasn't a bad thing, it was just life. And for over 20 years, I had forgotten this song. I don't believe I even sang it in the privacy of my home. As odd as this may seem, even odder was an unusual move of God in my life that took place a few years ago at my parents' 50th Anniversary weekend. On Sunday morning, all of us were gathered at my father's church to worship together with them and their church family. And on this special day, my father asked me right there in the middle of the song service, in front of everyone, if I would come up to the front and sing a special. I agreed, grabbed the songbook, and opened it up randomly. The pages fell onto...you guessed it...my old song! I must admit it took me back many years. I reared my head back and thought to myself, "Let's give

12

this thing a whirl for all it's worth!" I started out with that first verse and it seemed like an old familiar friend, one I hadn't seen in years, but the kind of friend you meet back up with and things just take up where you left off. It wasn't until I got to the chorus when it all hit me. The last 20 years of my life all flashed before me with one enormous wave of emotion. I couldn't even get the words out, "I know… God makes no mistakes." That was all it took. Those words which seemed so easy to sing as an adolescent and then later as a young woman with her whole life ahead of her were not so easy to sing as a woman of maturity who has had my share of hurts and disappointments in life. Yes, all of this is running fast-forward through my head as I was trying to gain control of my emotions so I could at least finish the chorus. I didn't blame my childish naivety because then, I was a mere child who knew nothing of the pains and woes of the real world. "I know God makes no mistakes" were the words I had sung all those years before, but with no connection. I had no major life experiences to back up what I would so emphatically and boldly proclaim in that song. Needless to say, I got through the song, but I questioned "Why, why, why did I almost lose it over this song? Don't I still believe, God makes no mistakes?" As I thought through that question, I had a crisis of confusion. Maybe I don't really believe it anymore? Am I having a crisis of faith? Or is this a mid-life crisis? If God really loves me then He had to make a mistake when He gave us our special needs daughter I finally admitted it to myself. I think that must have been the root conflict that was imbedded deep into my heart.

I had to take several days to process that entire experience. I evaluated every second, from the point I was asked to sing, to the point the song was randomly, or divinely chosen, to the point of my self-awareness that there was the possibility my dogmatic belief system had just been challenged to the core!

It doesn't surprise me now that God used a song, my song, to get my attention. He wanted me to lean into Him and wrestle out some confusion in my heart I didn't even realize was deeply rooted in the very depth of my soul. Greater still, He wanted me to know Him more. So, the wrestling began.

After several weeks had passed, I sat in the school car line waiting to pick up my son when an old radio broadcast came across the airwaves. Taped in the early 90's, I was quite reluctant to listen, yet as the woman tenderly shared her story, I was drawn to her every word. I just couldn't turn the channel. As I listened to her story of faith and courage, I couldn't help but think this woman's story is strangely similar to mine.

One word after the other, as she spoke, I related to her journey and each disappointment along the way. In the end, I sat in my mini-van with tears streaming down my face in awe of the grace God had so richly and favorably given to me. With a renewed zeal, I knew I wanted to share more of how God embraces me into His arms and gets me through each and every day.

I know what God had brought me through, and by His daily grace is getting me through, **is** a significant journey. It's a journey He was telling me needed to be shared. He required even more of my story than I had already so publicly shared. So, I said yes, sort of. I guess, I really bargained with God. I committed that day to God I would pursue writing my full story if only He would use it to help those who are hurting to find healing and hope in the loving arms of Jesus.

I am not into digging up old wounds! I like leaving well enough alone. Don't you? Well, God had other plans.

You see, I'm just a mom, like many of you, who is trying to love her family, whose husband happens to be a pastor, with a story to share. It's a story of loss, a story of love, and a story of learning how to lean into Jesus.

As we share together through this journey, you will discover the book of Ephesians uniquely mirrors my life and maybe even your life as well. My prayer is you will find yourself in the story, both my story and God's story, and in the end, you will know *God loves you this much*!

Questions For Reflection:
Have you ever had an experience that rocked your belief system to the core?

Have you been able to see God in the experience?

Can you think of a hurtful time in your life? Have you been able to heal from that hurt?

If you have been able to heal, how did it happen? What would you share with someone else going through the hurt you experienced?

Sometimes life passes so quickly you don't have time to reflect upon your experiences. The destination becomes the drive, when in reality, life should be more about the journey than the destination.

At my parent's 50th Anniversary, I had time to reflect back upon my life as my siblings and I celebrated our parents' lives and their 50 years together. These God-ordained events prompted me to dig even deeper into my life and I considered just how quickly time was flying past. I took several months to reflect upon my life, specifically my journey with God and others. I had to focus on WHY I was feeling like God didn't love me very much, and I had to re-evaluate who I was at my very core.

Ephesians talks a lot about who we are. Let's read this passage together.

> "[1]Paul, an apostle of Christ Jesus by the will of God, To God's holy people in Ephesus the faithful in Christ Jesus: [2]Grace and peace to you from God our Father and the Lord Jesus Christ. [3]Praise be to the God and Father of our Lord Jesus Christ, who has blessed us in the heavenly realms with every spiritual blessing in Christ. [4]For he chose us in him before the creation of the world to be holy and blameless in his sight. In love [5]he predestined us for adoption to sonship through Jesus Christ, in accordance with his pleasure and will— [6]to the praise of his glorious grace, which he has freely given us in the One he loves. [7]In him we have redemption through his blood, the forgiveness of sins, in accordance with the riches of God's grace [8]that he lavished on us. With all wisdom and understanding." (Ephesians 1:1-8)

Did you catch the significant truths of this passage? Even before God made the world, God loved us! If that were not enough, God chose us!

With the world full of rejection and heartache, I am so thankful I can have the assurance I have been chosen. No matter what life throws at me, I am wanted! Sometimes we just need to know this.

Catch the next wonderful thought. We are not simply loved and chosen by God, we are positioned by God. WE have a place. Through the awesome work of the cross, Jesus paved the way for us to be seen by God, not as we are, but as He is. He is holy and blameless before God. Do you realize we are not without fault? We are sinful, broken people, but because of Jesus, we are "without fault" in God's eyes. It doesn't say God chose us and

loved us because of our position and because we now look faultless and holy before Him. It says in Romans 5:8,
"But God demonstrates his own love for us in this: While we were still sinners, Christ died for us."

Our position has been purchased! We are adopted into royalty.

Loved, chosen, and royalty adopted. *We* are *wanted*! And this adoption was not a decision out of "last resource" or desperation, although we are desperately in need of a Savior. This adoption was decided in advance as stated in the KJV version. We have been predestined unto this adoption. In the Greek the word is proorizō (with rolled "r" in the first syllable: pro-ri-zo) which means to predetermine, decide beforehand.[2] *You* are *His first choice*! We are the First Lady. We are the Queen Mum! And at the final wedding feast, we will not just watch the royal wedding nor be in the bridal party, we will be the princess "Bride of Christ." What a truth for us to grasp!

There is so much truth for us in this study of Ephesians and I am so thrilled you are taking the time to study and grow together with me.

When life is lousy and you feel hopeless, remember you are a daughter of the King! When you are so low there is nowhere to turn but up, you are the princess bride! When your efforts seem useless, when your battles are raging, or when you feel unlovely or unloved, our Father wants you to know you are valuable. You are worth so much and you have a place and a position. You dear one, are loved!

One thing I want you to understand is I do not think my life is worse off than someone else. My mother said there is always, someone that is worse off than you. I know the very subject matter of my story and the title of our study will draw hurting women. I am deeply honored you are here. It takes so much courage to come out of the isolation loss inflicts upon us! To you who are enduring grief and heartache, take heart, this message is for you. I know God has brought you to this study for such a time as this in your life. I pray my lack of faith through my sufferings won't be a stumbling block to you, but God's Word will provide essential healing to your suffering soul.

And to those of you who have decided to join the study because it was the only study offered this time around, I pray you will open your hearts to His love, His leading, and you will lean into Jesus like never before.

This week you will study God's Word to really know who you are. Take time to re-evaluate your life, and bask in the truth that ***God loves you this much***!

2 HOPE AND LOSS

When we first learned we were going to have a child, our hearts were filled with excitement and anticipation. Like any parent, we wanted our first born to have the greatest life possible, a life full of hopes and dreams. Every mom wants the opportunity to tell her child, "You can be anything you want to be. The sky's the limit!" But what happens when your child has limitations? When their skies are not full of hopes and dreams? When, in fact, those dreams were dashed a long time ago; dashed with a diagnosis in a doctor's office - mildly, mentally retarded. The beautiful dream of what could and should be turned our beautiful dream into dust. And it is not just one dashed dream. What we experience is a series of little, lifelong losses. We know we have a blessed gift from God in our daughter Ashlyn, but the losses take their toll and can really make the day feel blue.

One of those losses came to us on the first day she went to school. For most moms, this day is filled with a lot of emotions. It is a huge milestone. With a special needs child, there is a loss because it is increasingly obvious our child isn't like the other kids. Our child rides the short yellow school bus. Our child goes to special classes. Our child is different.

Another loss came at church. I remember everyone else's daughters dressed up in their Sunday best because the children were singing in church for the first time. Our child wasn't dressed up. She wasn't singing. She was left playing in the classroom.

She won't go to prom, graduate from high school or college, or ever have her daddy walk her down the aisle.

If we do not recognize these losses as the source of our pain and work through them, we can become discouraged, emotionally drained, and even depressed. Believe me, I have been there.

On good days, Red, as I call Ashlyn because of her beautiful auburn hair, is fun, loving, thoughtful, and a joy to be around. On other days, she is a five-year-old in a grown-up body. Have you ever seen a 175-pound girl have a temper tantrum? When she is non-compliant these days, even daddy isn't big enough to make her comply.

These daily losses have become part of our everyday lives. We even make the statement, "It's Ashlyn's world; we're just living in it."

So, what do you do when you have a special needs child? You pray because when you are at the end of your rope, prayer is all that is left to do. You pray day in and day out because some days you just feel overwhelmed. Some days you even wonder if God is listening at all.

And some days you stir up enough faith to pray an audacious prayer, a bold prayer. You pray God would do the miraculous. You pray the prayer of Joshua. You remember the one? The prayer that God would make the sun stand still. You pray God would make the sun stand still for your child and for your situation. You just want, need, and long for the miraculous!

Sometimes God comes through and a little miracle emerges. Still, sometimes the prayer of faith is prayed day after day and the sun sets, despite your request. How do we reconcile our faith and our reality then? When we pray for the sun to stand still and the sun sets despite our best efforts, it feels like God has let us down, doesn't it? Let's talk about this important element of our prayer life, especially in seeing God do the miraculous in our lives.

Hebrews 11:1 says, "Now faith is being sure of what we hope for and certain of what we do not see."

In life, there are some things we can be sure about. And then, there are those hopes we just keep hoping for. When talking about faith and prayer we often hear this Bible verse quoted. "He was wounded for our transgressions...and by His stripes we are healed." (NKJV, Isaiah 53:5)

I believe this verse gives me confidence that we are healed by His precious stripes of blood. However, this version does not mean my every illness here on this earth is going to be healed. Sometimes, our loved ones pass from here into the presence of Jesus. We have assurance of this fact through the Scripture that says, "We are confident, I say, and would prefer to be away from the body and at home with the Lord." (2 Corinthians 5:8)

I believe it is much like the description of the second coming of Christ found in 1 Corinthians 15:52, our home going is like a blink, like "the twinkling of an eye."

So, yes, with confidence I believe by His stripes we are healed. As Christians, we often hope and pray for an earthly healing, yet what could be a better healing than your next breath being in the very presence of our loving, Heavenly Father? It is not some kind of prayer or faith failure on our part when God chooses to bring a child home. This struggle of faith and failure has been mine many times. Maybe you have felt the same feelings? "Maybe if I prayed longer, harder, or more intensely? Maybe if I fasted and prayed God would answer my prayers my way."

God answered my feelings of failure regarding Ashlyn in a gentle reminder while I was right in the middle of a fast. I was spending a few moments in worship and listening to a song. The words were talking about "one day there would be no more pain or sorrow" (KJV, Revelation. 21:4) and how glorious that day would be. As I was singing along, praising and in awe of that thought, God interrupted my worship with a little "sidebar melody of His own." I honestly could not believe the thought He sent my way right in the middle of that praise. I know you are all dying to know, so here is what He said: "Yes, and there will be pain and sorrow on this earth until that day!"

What? So that's my answer, Lord? I had to stop and write those words down because despite my fasting, despite my Bible reading, this was all God had given me. And quite frankly after that moment, I went back to my Bible reading, hoping for another answer. I was earnestly seeking answers. I needed an answer from God as to what to do about Ashlyn's issues. I did NOT want the answer God gave me. So, I searched and searched and still nothing!

This is not the first time I have gotten a "no" from the Lord, but I am not going to give up hope. I am going to continue to have peace about the situation. It is rarely our lack of faith that is to blame when God says no; however, a no from God is tough to hear. This is especially true when God chooses to say, "No, I am going to heal that sickness only through a heavenly homecoming!" So, by His stripes, we are healed? Yes, but often an ultimate healing only occurs at the end of our lives here on earth.

I am so excited to share with you what I have learned through the study of Ephesians. We all need to cling to hope in our lives and Ephesians has much to teach us about hope. Let's dive in.

"[17]I keep asking that the God of our Lord Jesus Christ, the glorious Father, may give you the Spirit of wisdom and revelation, so that you may know him better. [18]I pray that the eyes of your heart may be enlightened in order that you may know the **hope** to which he has called you, the riches of his glorious inheritance in his holy people, [19]and his incomparably great power for us who believe. That power is the same as the mighty strength [20]he exerted when he raised Christ from the dead and seated him at his right hand in the heavenly realms, [21]far above all rule and authority, power and dominion, and every name that is invoked, not only in the present age but also in the one to come." (NIV, Ephesians 1:17-21) (emphasis mine)

We may have hopeless situations, but one hope is certain. At the end of our earthly journey, if we are in Christ, we have assurance our future is secure. We have an ultimate healing coming! Our hope is in this inheritance of eternal life. Yes, it stinks living on this earth sometimes, and our hurts run deep, but take heart because our battle has already been won. The Bible tells us our lives are like a vapor (James 4:14). We are here for such a short period of time, then like a vapor, our lives vanish away. So be sure and have conviction about this hope. One day we will have an ultimate healing.

As Christians our eternal hope is secure, but what about our hope for the here and now? The great news is we can find hope for our every loss and hope for our every gain right in the middle of the Bible. The Psalmists knew much about loss, but it is evident they knew even more about hope. Let's look at the Psalms for a few moments. These verses, taken from the New International Version, provide much instruction on hope. Let's read them thoughtfully, and chew on their meaning together.

"Guide me in your truth and teach me, for you are God my Savior, and my hope is in you all day long." (Psalm 25:5)

"May integrity and uprightness protect me, because my hope, LORD, is in you" (Psalm 25:21)

"But now, Lord, what do I look for? My hope is in you" (Psalm 39:7)

"Why, my soul, are you downcast? Why so disturbed within me? Put your hope in God, for I will yet praise him, my Savior and my God" (Psalm 42:5)

"Yes, my soul, find rest in God; my hope comes from him." (Psalm 62:5)

"Guide me in your truth and teach me, for you are God my Savior, and my hope is in you all day long." (Psalm 25:5)

When the losses of life strike us down, we are to seek out the truth about our loss. We need to accurately view our loss and then we are instructed to dwell on what God says about it. For example, I know in my head the truth about our every situation. Romans 8:28 says, "All things work together for good to those who love God", so the truth is whatever loss I am enduring is working to my good. This is true whether I feel like it is working or whether I like the outcome. Quite frankly, most of the time we don't like the outcome. If we liked it, we most likely would not consider it a loss, right?

Still, I don't have to like it to know it falls under all things, and God says He is working it out for my good. Now, my heart is most likely saying "this is not fair", or "why would God allow this to happen to me", or even the most dangerous of my lingering thoughts, "God must not love me very much to allow this to happen to me." When we know the truth about our loss

24

we are to dwell on that hope. And not just for that moment of the day, but it says to cling to that hope "all day long."

What do we do when we don't know what to do? When we are confused or have questions and don't know where to look? We declare as the Psalmist did in 39:7, "But now, Lord, what do I look for? My hope is in you."

God allows us to question if we ask the question to the right person! We can go to friends who may sympathize with our situation. They may even say nice things, but God will never give us a wrong answer about our loss. When we ask Him, "Ok, Lord, now what do I do?" Our answer is always, "Your hope is in me!"

When we are discouraged, when our soul is down and disturbed and even depressed, the Bible instructs us to put our hope in God. Did you notice how the Psalmist speaks to his heart? He recognized his own feelings. He is depressed, discouraged, and down. Then he tells his feelings and his heart what to do. "Put your hope in God!" But, he doesn't stop there. He then praises God! Praise should always come next.

When you are downhearted, praise is the best medicine for your soul. Believe me, I know from experience. My waistline would really appreciate it if I would exercise praise instead of my chocolate indulgence!

Ask yourself this question, "What do I do when I feel down?"

Whatever your answer, instead of that behavior, tell yourself to put your hope in God and then start praising Him.

Don't be confused by the Scripture. Read it in context. If you stop at Psalm 39, you may fail to see the promise of hope. The Psalmist in chapter 39 does not have a defined word of assurance, even in reading through to the end of the entire Psalm. So how does placing our hope in God help our hopeless situation? Here it is, the last resort, the last, ditch effort of desperation. When there is nowhere else to turn, the Psalmist is at his lowest; he has only hope left. This is our hope - that we **can** have hope! Then, the 40th Psalm is full of the guarantee of peace, the peace that accompanies our praise. That is a guarantee you can count on!

Finally, when we learn to place our hope in the Lord, when we learn to praise God in whatever our circumstances, then we can rest in the Lord. According to our last Psalm, Psalm 65:5, we can speak to ourselves. Get your feelings in line with your head and your heart will follow. Tell yourself you are resting on God because your hope is not in yourself. Our hope is not in man. Our hope is not in medical science. Our hope is not in the "if only this would happen" or "if I could do this or that," our hope comes from Him and we hope in Him!

Through the losses and through the wins, one constant remains, my faith walk. It is hope. I can endure almost anything if I have hope God is with me and for me. I'm not going to listen to the naysayers who are sure Red will never be totally potty-trained. Don't take away my hope. I reject those who tell me it can't happen. My hope is in an all-powerful God. I do not know how much God will allow Ashlyn to accomplish, but I know He is able. **I need hope when everything seems impossible; I need hope my prayer is possible.**

Regardless of how God answers, there is one thing of which I am certain, my hope rests in the Lord. It is His business and, as hard as life may be, He is allowing it to work together for my good and Red's good. Whatever He is allowing to happen to you, He is working it all for your good, too.

The Bible teaches "faith is the substance of things hoped for, the evidence of things not yet seen." This is such a powerful truth to us today because, while we are placing all of our hope in the Lord, we expect the Lord to move or make something happen on our behalf, whether it is a financial loss, or a family loss, or a physical loss. Maybe your hope is for gain and not loss. Perhaps you are hoping for a gain in spiritual growth for your family, a gain in financial growth for your situation, or a gain in your relationships. When we study the Bible we are activating our faith by an act of our will, both inwardly and outwardly by our walk and our words. We are believing what is not seen will be seen. Even when we are weary, we shouldn't give up hope and we shouldn't fail in faith, even when our physical bodies want to give up.

The prophet Zechariah knew about the obstacle of weariness in well-doing. The angel of the Lord gave him this encouragement, and this same verse came to my mind as I was preparing to encourage you, "Not by might, nor by power but by my spirit, says the Lord Almighty." (Zechariah 4:6 NIV) The prophet was weary and his spirit was fainting when he was given his marching orders. He didn't want to give the bad news and he was the prophet! Matthew Henry's Commentary says this on the passage:

"What comes from the grace of God, may, in faith, be committed to the grace of God, for he will not forsake the work of his own hands."[3]

However, you are feeling about your lot in life, it is not by might or power you will get through it. It is by the Spirit of God. It is His job and His responsibility. He is responsible for the how in our lives. When He calls us to a task He will accomplish the task. Of that, you can be sure.

While our hope is in the Lord, we still need to stir our faith up! What we are hoping will not come by our human might or some human power, but by God's Spirit. "For He Who began a good work in you, will be faithful to complete it." (Philippians 1:6) As we walk in faith, we place our hope in the Lord and rest in Him. He is not going to forsake us or the work He has started in us.

When all hope is gone, if we place our hope in God despite our circumstances, God is pleased with our faith. We are not faith failures because God tells us "no" or "not yet" in our lives, but we do need to know how to respond to that answer.

Raising a special needs child can be all consuming at times. I do question why God would give us such a responsibility along with the ministry of pastoring a church. It is not easy. The feelings of loss are a constant strain draining our emotional and physical strength. Although Red's disabilities are prominent in our lives, they do not define us. I never want to be known for the problems, but I do want to be known for the promises God has fulfilled in my life! God has given her to us, as a gift. I know God uses the challenges of raising a special child to develop us, not to harm us, and to give us a hope and a future!

If your emotional tank is low or your physical strength is waning, I understand how the losses in your life can be draining you in every area of life. I pray your pain or problem will not define you either, but that you will be known for standing on the promises of God through your situation.

Questions For Reflection:
What loss or losses have you endured?

Have you had to let someone who you love dearly go to that ultimate healing?

Can you identify how your reaction to the loss has affected you?

What part did God play in your reactions or responses?

At that time in your life, if God was not a part of your worldview, do you believe He would have made a difference? How?

What about hope? What are you hoping for?

And how does hope encourage us on our faith journey?

Have you ever felt as if your pain or loss has defined you?

Can you identify how your pain or loss drains your life? Do you think you are wired to be more drained physically, spiritually, or emotionally?

Think about how you can renew these depleted areas of your life?

My prayer is God will use this study to encourage and strengthen you as you walk through the disappointments and losses in your life. I pray you will put your hope in the Lord, your faith will grow strong, and you will know it is His work in and through you.

We will now focus on the second half of Ephesians 1. There is so much to know. We will continue learning how to place our hope in the Lord and lean into Jesus. Study diligently and know, **God loves you this much!**

3 BABY LOSS

Wrestling with God over the loss of raising a special child, Ashlyn, turned out to be a significant part of my life. Still, I know the loss of our babies, which seems like a lifetime ago now, is huge in my journey to fully know God loves me, so please pardon my writing my story out of order.

As a young child, I recall my desire to be a mother was very strong. I would not only play dolls, I would dress, clean, and feed my baby dolls. I would pray God would give me a live baby to love, care for, and nurture. I remember one particular night. I prayed and prayed to God I would awaken in the morning and a little baby would just be lying in my doll baby's crib. You remember those cribs, so small your fake baby doll would barely fit, let alone a real infant! Still, I kept it right next to my bed and prayed for a miracle. Of course, I was greatly disappointed when I awoke the next morning to find only that stiff lifeless plastic doll lying in my real baby's place. I admitted earlier I am somewhat of a dreamer. Even as I write about this part of my life, it seems so ridiculous. Still, I guess it just emphasizes the fact I am highly imaginative! There is no harm in a few fantastic fantasies, is there? It is just the artist in me, I guess.

Yet one thing I am certain of, the motherly instinct was instilled deep within me even when I was very young. As my days flew into adolescence and young adulthood, I remember one of my deepest desires transitioned from mommyhood to being in love. Maybe I was in love with the idea of being in love more than I really loved the few steady boyfriends I had. But God knew in order for me to finish college before I got married, He would have to keep all the guys I had my eyes on away from me. And as God always does with God things, He did a very good job of it. I didn't really date at all during my college years, at least not until I met the love of my life.

During my senior year of college, I finally met the man of my dreams.

We married, and God began to fulfill my heart's greatest desires. My man not only loves me, but he loves God with a passion and fervor I admire most in him. My man makes life full of fun and laughter. I put my secret childhood desire to become a mom on hold for a few years as a bigger dream became my purpose. This bigger dream was to get my hubby through Bible College. You see, if young dreamers were honest, we would admit our goal, first and foremost, is to change the world. For me, that was my goal. Only my worldview is so strongly influenced by God and the Bible, my goal became, "What does God want me to do that will change the world?" Only now, my goal was no longer my goal. In what seemed like a twinkling of a moment, I went from my goal, my dreams to our goals, our dreams. The first few years of our marriage were fairy-tale in nature. Bits and pieces of it were flawed, as we were two selfish characters who were very self-centered and strong-willed. This combination didn't fly sometimes. When life and our selfish desires interfered with God's plans and purposes for our lives, most of the time we took the easy way out and ignored our differences. We didn't really work intentionally on our marriage. We would move from conflict to peace without really resolving our self-centeredness and without really working on changing our relationship. This unhealthy way of living did not do us well as we started to enter a phase of loss in our young marriage.

The first loss was difficult in that we had hoped and prayed and waited for over a year to finally get pregnant. Many can relate to the process and the pain of hurrying to the pharmacy to buy a pregnancy stick and the great anticipation each month as you read the results. I recall staring hopelessly at the single pink line. I began believing if I held it long enough, if I stared at it long enough, maybe, just maybe I would see a glimmer of a double pink line in the stick. Each month brought disappointment as the reality I would have to wait another month to try to get pregnant would hit me like a ton of emotional bricks! I know Paul was not quite as disappointed each month. I guess most men are never overly anxious to have their first child. At least he didn't express his disappointment, and so I felt alone during those times

When we finally did get pregnant a year later, we were quickly disappointed by a traumatic first loss. Our first pregnancy was a tubal pregnancy. The doctor got very upset with my resistance to just simply follow protocol and end the pregnancy. I had started spotting in my sixth week, and I went to the doctor's office to have an ultrasound. He determined the pregnancy looked like it was in the tubes, and he thought he could save my tube with a new laparoscopic surgery in which he just happened to specialize. I wasn't quite as concerned about saving my fallopian tube. I was concerned with saving my baby! In fact, I had my husband question the doctor so we were absolutely, positively sure, beyond any shadow of a doubt the baby was indeed in the tubes and not a viable pregnancy. Since tubal pregnancies are highly dangerous and can be fatal to the mother, the doctor was not very happy with our apprehensions. "Baby Tubal" was our first glimpse of parenthood. It will never be forgotten. Although short lived, this baby brought us much joy. Baby Tubal was a wonder and even though he didn't make it to the safety of my womb, we believe he is in the arms of Jesus.

Amazingly, God perfectly timed our loss. So perfect, in fact, He was immediately able to use our loss right where we were. Our church had scheduled a special drama group, and they had planned to perform a dramatic piece that dealt precisely with the issue of a couple facing the loss of a baby and their response. This was no coincidence. This was a comfort to us at the time, but I was really ready for a change in our situation. My faith was strong in my youth and I knew in my head God makes no mistakes. So, I acted upon what I knew to be truth. I simply gave my grief over to my Lord and rested in the fact He does know what is best. I had hoped our first loss would pave the way for what the Lord had for our life's purpose as a family.

Thankfully, change came almost too soon and our grief was short-lived. We wasted no time hoping to get pregnant again and our hope was strong. As God planned, we became pregnant the very next month. Filled with hope and anticipation, we anxiously waited out that three-month safety term. We felt if we could get through the first three months, the baby would be born and our hopes and dreams would finally begin to be fulfilled.

Soon the long months of waiting were over. Through a rough and risky emergency C-section, our little redheaded porcelain doll was born. She was 5 pounds 14 ½ ounces and born right on her due date, March 3, 1996. She had congenital hip dislocation in both hips. Her little legs were breech in the womb for so many months she needed to be in a Velcro harness for her first five months. For this reason, we were not overly concerned when she didn't seem to reach all of the physical benchmarks most babies reach. She also had very low muscle tone and had we had our son first, we would have realized something just wasn't quite right with her. Still, even with all that was going on with little Ashlyn Rebecca, we had a desire to try for another baby.

With Ashlyn about two years old, off we went. We seemed to get pregnant a lot easier this time around and we were full of hope. When the seven-week check-up came around, the doctor struggled to find a heartbeat. He encouraged us not to worry, explaining sometimes the baby is earlier than first thought and it may just be too early to hear the heartbeat. Still, as though we were waking up to some rewind of our life that was way too familiar, more tests were taken. I knew this time the possibility of miscarriage was very real. We hadn't heard the heartbeat and the hormone levels came back lower than normal in the following weeks. It was hard to hear that report. I knew the next step was to make the dreaded appointment at the hospital. We were scheduled for a D & C the next morning. I remember breaking down that afternoon in the shower, sobbing over the loss of our second little baby. This baby I remember fondly as our Baby November. He was harder to lose than the others, not because I loved him more, but because I saw him more clearly. I always wanted to make sure science and medicine were not in error and we were really making the right decisions. I just wanted to make sure the baby was not living. Since the baby was nine weeks at this time, the doctor turned the ultrasound picture around and showed us our Baby November. This picture will stay with me forever. I am sure of it. The lifeless baby was swollen a bit because he was already starting to decompose. Seeing this baby like this drove home the reality of the life that was and the life that was lost. A baby we didn't hold in our arms or hear breathe, but a little peanut we saw with our eyes, another one precious to us and precious to God. The main thought that got me through that night was the truth God thought this baby just as precious as all babies born. God knew his formation in the womb just as the Scripture in Psalm 132 states.

I had yet another moment with God where I gave that baby over to His perfect will and way. I knew Baby November was safely cradled in the arms of my heavenly Father, and I was okay with that picture.

I didn't struggle too much with the loss. I just kept my heart and head aligned with the truth of the Sovereignty of God in my life. I knew the Scriptures applied to my life concerning all of these things.

Jeremiah 29:11 says "For I know the plans I have for you declares the Lord, plans to prosper and not to harm you." Right? Again, this loss was followed by another attempt to increase our little family. We questioned how much loss a couple could endure and yet still be courageous enough to keep our faith in the sovereignty of God's perfect plan and purpose for our lives. Within a few months, another pregnancy had renewed us with hope once again. By the time Easter had rolled around, we were expecting again. I remember the morning of Easter Sunday so vividly. I was leading our church choir and so thrilled with the music and rejoicing on that special Sunday. I started to get choked up and could barely rehearse. I said, "It is probably the hormones!" Everyone laughed. Little did I know my feeling so good that day was not a good sign. I was only about eight weeks along and I felt little to no morning sickness. By the end of the next week, we had troubling indications yet another baby may be in jeopardy. This baby was my spring baby. And, yes, we lost Baby Spring that week, too. The loss back to back with Baby November just seemed too great to endure at the time. As they rolled me into that now all too familiar operating room, in that little Virginia hospital (a hospital I came to dread even passing on the road), I could not help but begin to cry. And yet as the tears were streaming down my face, God came near to me in a strange and comforting way. In the holding room of that operating room, a gentle, elderly man came over to my bed and held my hand. He didn't even have to say a word. His presence was all that I needed. It was like God himself, dressed up in

36

human grandpa form, had come to hold my hand until I dosed off to sleep from the anesthesia. I can't remember our exchange or if he prayed, I just vaguely remember his smile and his comforting voice saying, "it will be alright." It was alright. Just like it always is.

The loss of these babies pose an unusual question today, one our culture increasingly treats with a cold reality. Just how much should we grieve over the loss of an unborn child?

We are going to dive into our study discussing the sovereignty of God in our lives and our responses when we experience grievous loss.

In our study passage this week, Ephesians 2:8-10, we have instruction concerning God's will for our lives. Even when we don't understand God's will, we can rest in what we do know, His Word. Ephesians 2:8-10 says, "[8]For it is by grace you have been saved, through faith-and this not from yourselves, it is the gift of God- [9]not by works, so that no one can boast. [10]For we are God's workmanship, created in Christ Jesus to do good works, which God prepared in advance for us to do."

I believe God knows us so well He knew we would constantly struggle with who is in control of our lives. And certainly, He knew we would question the whys in our lives. Although the Christian thing to do would be to state, "Oh yes! I believe God is in control," we all know we really would like to be in control most of the time. In this passage, we see God kind of puts us in our place.

In His gentle yet wise manner, Our Father firmly makes it clear to us who claim to be followers, we are not to boast, brag, or even snicker about who has done the saving here. We are reminded we are in need of grace and it is God's free gift. We are the recipients of His grace. There is nothing good enough for us to in any way earn this salvation on our own. It was only through the work of the cross Jesus endured for us!

It is no wonder verse 10 emphasizes to us the idea we are His. We belong to Him. Read verse 10 again. "For we are God's masterpiece. He has created us anew in Christ Jesus, so we can do the good things he planned for us long ago." We are His masterpiece. He is the creator and we are the created.

God created all of them, each and every life we lost: Baby Tubal, Baby November, and Baby Spring. They were each formed in my womb or tube. God knows these babies, and each child was created with a plan God designed before time began. Those babies were never really mine. They were and are His.

As we consider the Sovereignty of God in our lives, it is imperative we remember who we are and whose we are.

In choosing who and what He desires for our lives, it is to our advantage to align our hopes with His hopes, our dreams with His dreams, and our desires, with what He so desires.

So, what about the grief? Since God is sovereign and we know in our heads our loss was allowed by God, then what about our hearts?

Can someone please relay this truth in my head to my hurting heart?

If we get nothing else out of this study today, I truly believe God wants us to know it is right for us to grieve for our unborn babies.

As I sat in that parking lot and listened to the story of the woman, a story God used to get my attention about sharing all of this, a second instruction was revealed to me. "We must acknowledge the loss of these babies."

If we don't, who will?

Our culture is constantly screaming at us that our babies were not viable lives. But the Bible tells us "They were known by God." They were known even from the beginning of time, just like you and I who have been born. God had a plan and a purpose for them. I love the quote my friends used when they wanted to honor and acknowledge to the world their baby mattered and was a life too soon lost. They had magnets made to hand out to those who attended their memorial service. Their baby, Baby Jude, was stillborn. The magnet had a picture of his little newborn foot and the quote was, "There is no foot so small that it cannot leave an imprint on this world." We need to recognize their lives and the loss of their lives while still knowing that "God is light and there is no darkness in him at all." (NIV, 1 John 1:5b)

You see, we are to grieve. Still, the Bible is very clear about one thing. We do not grieve as one who has no hope.

"[13]Brothers and sisters, we do not want you to be uninformed about those who sleep in death, so that you do not grieve like the rest of mankind, who have no hope. [14]For we believe that Jesus died and rose again, and so we believe that God will bring with Jesus those who have fallen asleep in him. [15]According to the Lord's word, we tell you that we who are still alive, who are left until the coming of the Lord, will certainly not precede those who have fallen asleep. [16]For the Lord himself will come down from heaven, with a loud command, with the voice of the archangel and with the trumpet call of God, and the dead in Christ will rise first. [17]After that, we who are still alive and are left will be caught up together with them in the clouds to meet the Lord in the air. And so we will be with the Lord forever. [18]Therefore encourage one another with these words." (NIV, 1 Thessalonians 4:13-18)

Let me encourage you today. At that final hour, we will be caught up together. We will be joined with all of our loved ones, and we will be with the Lord forever! Now that is a hope you can depend upon!

Questions For Reflection:

If you have lost a child, how have you dealt with your loss?

What does the Bible say about loss and grief?

How can our community of believers minister most effectively to those that have experienced these kinds of losses?

Dry your tears for now, because we grieve with hopeful hearts, knowing one day we will see those beautiful babies, and they couldn't be in safer arms than Jesus.

They are His after all.

4 SUGAR AND SPICE

Sugar and spice and everything nice. Are these not the things of which little girls are made? Still, at least a few times a week, I struggle with questioning God about our special daughter. This is my story of continual loss…and my battle with the sovereignty of God. My hope is you find some nuggets of truth to help guide you on your faith journey. God has led me to some awesome discoveries in the Book of Ephesians that help me as I battle. The only way I know how to address this issue of continual loss and on-going faith struggles is to take you on the journey Paul and I encounter in our lives on a daily basis.

"A Day In The Life of Ashlyn…"

You know, God has always been so gracious to us in our lives. He is always *on time*. He may not answer when I want HIM to answer. His answer may not always be the answer I am looking for, but I am certain He is always right on time. At just the right time, God eased us into the realization Ashlyn was not going to be like all the other kids, and our lives were going to look very different from what we had envisioned. Ashlyn is not just developmentally delayed. The sore news is Ashlyn is mildly, mentally handicapped.

For the people who very delicately ask about Ashlyn, and for those who ignore the fact she is handicapped because they are too embarrassed to ask, I try to explain her condition simply and concisely and in terms I feel are universally understood.

Raising Ashlyn is much like living with Rain Man, Radio, and I am Sam all wrapped up into one beautiful curly haired redhead!

Ashlyn continues to be a blessing. She is also a challenge each and every day of our lives. I say that with great reserve, but the truth is a special needs child is like having a life sentence without the possibility of parole! Yeah, I had to stop and think to myself what you most likely are thinking right now, too. "Is that okay to say out loud?"

When a close mentor of mine made this harsh statement referring to life with her typical, adult kids, I cringed at first. Ultimately, I had to admit she is spot on! I mean, even when our kids are typical, even when they are grown, we as parents celebrate every joy and suffer every heartache our children experience. Parenting, regardless of the circumstances, is a life sentence without the possibility of parole.

It is tough enough to explain what life is like when raising a special needs child without feeling as if I have to sugar coat it. So, at the risk of severely offending some people, I am just going to continue to be brutally honest. I love our daughter tremendously and I wouldn't give her up for anything in the world, but it is very tough every day.

Raising Ashlyn is a daunting task; an endeavor I never would wish on anyone, even my worst enemies. The mental trauma and daily drama are sometimes unbearable. I speak this in all sincerity and truth. Some days you get "Special Ashlyn" and those days she is compliant, jovial and very pleasant. Other days you get "Needy Ashlyn." Unfortunately, the demanding neediness of Ashlyn can be enough to make a grown man cry!

Literally!!!

Ask her dad!

Yet, each and every day we find ourselves going to sleep in peace and waking up to face another day with peace on our side. Not because we have gained peace for Ashlyn, but because we live in the constant protection of "The Prince of Peace-Jesus!" It is not our optimal plan, but neither is it our Plan B. We rely totally on God as our Plan A because it is God's Plan A for our family. Ashlyn is a joy, and I love her dearly. She adds so much to our lives.

There is certainly no monotony with Ashlyn. While her routine is predictable, her temperament is not. Simply put, Ashlyn can be a brat at times. It is as if we are stuck living with the terrible twos our entire life. The only difference is the toddler is now 5'5 and 170 pounds! She can throw a fit and meltdown as fast as any two-year-old. If she gets her mind set on what or how she will do something, you can guarantee that is how it is going to be. The best litigation lawyer cannot change her mind. I am not one to reason too much with a two-year-old but sometimes I forget and try to reason with my now 21-year old daughter. Despite her actual age, reasoning with Ashlyn is like trying to persuade the sun not to rise or the ocean not to draw back its tides. Whatever she opposes, she ends up verbally hating. When she is not getting her way, her booming voice rises and those strong arms cross in defiance, just like a rap artist expressing angry lyrics. Finally, she storms across the room in a rage and then the tantrum ends in a huff and a puff and usually prompts a like response from one of us. And yes, her behavior is unpredictable and completely unstoppable.

The flip side is the fact you get to have a two-year-old with you forever. You will never have to experience the empty nest. You always have a child-filled, whimsical Christmas. You know, the kind where it doesn't matter what is inside the present. The joy is found in the simple fact she gets to open a present! My particularly favorite joy is knowing I will always have a willing partner to go with me to Disney World and ride "Peeper" Pan, as she so endearingly calls the ride through Never Neverland.

Who wouldn't love to live with a real-life Napoleon Dynamite? It would seem she has taken cues and expression lessons right from the movie itself. Guyshhhhh….what a G?" I don't even know what that means????

There is a misconception special needs kids are always so sweet, lovable, and funny. And, they are. But, they are also the polar opposites of those traits sometimes. One of our main struggles is the "Battle in the Bathroom!" Ashlyn still has to be coerced to perform simple tasks related to hygiene. Even coercion does not always result in success. If you are in those potty-training days (or have lived through them), I am sure you understand my frustration. Now, imagine living in that stage for over 21 looooonnnnngggggg years!

While we have experienced a great deal of progress with Ashlyn, she still holds onto behavior rooted in rebellion. "I don't want to do it!" is a response all too familiar to those in Ashlyn's world.

I think God must laugh at me and my frustration with Ashlyn. Isn't rebellion the sole heart problem of the human race? We are constantly saying, "I don't want to!" Aren't we? We are all like little two-year-olds telling God "no."

Just like any conflict, we fight and yell at each other trying to get Ashlyn to do what is right and healthy for her. It is not a pretty picture and a far cry from the peaceful home atmosphere I would love to have but can only imagine in our home. I dream of "Leave It to Beaver" or "Little House on the Prairie," but the situation is much more like "The Simpsons."

Not to belabor this topic, but one of my biggest fears, and one I experience daily is the fear Ashlyn will never be completely potty-trained. My fear comes from the knowledge this is a very real possibility. Still, I see glimpses of progress occasionally, so I refuse to give up hope. This battle drains me emotionally like no other.

I rest in the hope God is able and may perform this miracle in her life one day. Until then, I pray my faith will get me through the battle.

I just know an answer to this simple request would make life so much easier for all of us.

Then I wonder if that is a fair prayer? Is it a prayer to make my life easier? Are selfish prayers fair to ask of the Lord? There is a loss in that moms of special needs kids are often reduced from mother to maidservant. As mothers, we are all our children's maidservants for a time, but most mothers get the opportunity to outgrow this phase, but those of us who parent special needs children most likely will not.

The confusing question is, "What does God want me to do?" Pray more? Confess more? Acknowledge His power and presence more? Or, are prayers that ask to make our lives easier wrong? Am I wrong? These are just some of the questions I battle with on a reoccurring basis.

Raising a special needs child is not much different from raising a difficult child or a strong-willed child. The main exception is her understanding of consequences and right and wrong are not easily ascertained. As she has matured, there is no doubt Ashlyn has grown into understanding consequences to a certain degree. Her level of intelligence limits some of her understanding beyond the concrete concepts in life. This cognitive limitation makes many simple tasks difficult.

What about you? What challenges do you face on a daily basis? Is there anything in your life that seems like a daily battle?

Whether or not you have a special needs child or you are experiencing a trial that is of a totally different nature, I like what Francis Chan says about life's circumstances in his book, Crazy Love. "It is easy to become disillusioned with the circumstances of our lives compared to others. But in the presence of God, He gives us deeper peace and joy that transcends it all. To be brutally honest, it doesn't really matter what place you find yourself in right now our sole point in life is to point to God."[4] Whether you are dealing with a strong-willed child, suffering through a debilitating illness, or you are trying to get a 21-year old potty-trained, our chief goal in life is to point to God.

For this reason, I have to come to peace with the fact that this is God's perfect plan for my life and He wants me to glorify Him through every aspect of it. I admit, I don't always act like I have this peace, but I can make the choice to point to Jesus in the "whatsoever I do in my life," or, I can point to myself and become self-absorbed. Do I want others to have a pity-party because of the trials in my life or do I want them to see the strength God gives me to live through the trials of raising a special needs child?

What are some of your issues? You know, those little life chores that seem so meaningless? How do you really feel about being a mother? Does the idea of staying home to raise the kids and not be able to contribute to the family income make you crazy sometimes? I know I have dealt with that issue a lot over my life. Even when I know the job of a stay-at-home mom is one that is vitally important in the lives of our kids, it still seems at times to be dull and monotonous at best! Maybe you are on the flip side of the coin. Do you have feelings of guilt because you do work outside the home and you would give anything to stay at home with your kids? How does the monotony of the daily job make you feel? It is tough to be a mom and work outside of the home. I don't care if you are Wonder Woman!

I don't know what it is you are facing today. I do know each and every day we all have choices to make. We can embrace our problems and see the opportunity to lean in closer to Jesus. Or, we can allow our problem to make us bitter, depressed and hopeless.

Whatever situation we find ourselves in today, we all have the capacity within us to be bitter, bitter about the life God has us in right now.

While we are in the midst of these problems the Bible can bring such comfort. Here are some of my favorite verses for troubled times.

The Bible says, "Come near to God and he will come near to you." (James 4:8a). I can take comfort He is near when I am in need. You, too, can take comfort from that today. He is not far away. He is close.

Consider Matthew 25:40b, "whatever you did for one of the least of these brothers and sisters of mine, you did for me."

This verse gives me value as I serve as unto the Lord and not unto man or unto Ashlyn! Your little toddler is the least of these. When you change that stinky diaper for the umpteenth time, you are doing this as unto the Lord. When you change your elderly parent's bedpan, you are doing this as unto the Lord! Whatever it is that may make you feel less than what God intends, if you are serving as unto the Lord, you are doing it as if the Lord is the one you are serving.

Finally, Colossians 3:17 says, "And whatever you do, whether in word or deed, do it all in the name of the Lord Jesus, giving thanks to God the Father through him."

This verse comforts me when I feel as if I am doing the mundane with no purpose or rhyme or reason. In the doldrums of life, we can glorify God!

These Scriptures are such a daily comfort to me when I am in the middle of a battle. However, as comforting as these words are to me, I cannot overemphasize the power of Ephesians 3:17-19 (NIV). "[17]so that Christ may dwell in your hearts through faith. And I pray that you, being rooted and established in love, [18]may have power, together with all the Lord's holy people, to grasp how wide and long and high and deep is the love of Christ, [19]and to know this love that surpasses knowledge—that you may be filled to the measure of all the fullness of God."

This text is at the heart of our entire study of Ephesians. Let's look at it once more in The Amplified Version:

[17]so that Christ may dwell in your hearts through your faith. And may you, having been [deeply] rooted and [securely] grounded in love, [18]be fully capable of comprehending with all the saints (God's people) the width and length and height and depth of His love [fully experiencing that amazing, endless love]; [19]and [that you may come] to know [practically, through personal experience] the love of Christ which far surpasses [mere] knowledge [without experience], that you may be filled up [throughout your being] to all the fullness of God [so that you may have the richest experience of God's presence in your lives, completely filled and flooded with God Himself]. (Ephesians 3;17-19)

I believe I can get through almost anything if I am sold on this one truth. I find it right here in this text: God loves me this much!!!

I know this love is extravagant. It is wide enough to span my every trial, my every circumstance. Nothing is beyond the boundaries of God's great love for me. It is long. It is never-ending. It never runs out! God's love for me is deep. Can you grasp that image? Nothing I can say or do is so bad that God's love can't reach down and pull me up! Finally, God's extravagant love for us is so high it is beyond us. We cannot comprehend or understand this dimension of God's love for us. However, we can experience these dimensions of His love and we need to know beyond a shadow of a doubt God loves me this much!!!

You see we each have the potential to take our losses in life and become bitter people. We all have experienced losses that have the ability to overshadow our lives. And yet we are given a choice every day as to how we will respond. We all have the natural inclination to feel we are being treated unfairly. We can grow hard and cold. We may even begin to believe God must not love me very much! I felt that way not so long ago, but then I considered God's love for me, whose I am and who He is, and where my hope must lie, I had a choice to make!

I can live bitter or I can get better.

Questions For Reflection:
Do you understand how bitterness works against us all?

So, what is your Ashlyn-style problem? Maybe you are not raising a special needs child, but chances are you have a similar situation in some aspect of your life in which you struggle.

Maybe your issue is sickness, a job choice, or a difficult relationship? Whatever your issue, have you come to accept your circumstances may be God's Plan A for your life...His perfect will for you?

What about love? Do you fully understand the depth, length, and breadth of God's great love for you?

Getting better means that when I choose to bask in the extravagant, unending love of God in my every circumstance in life, then I can get through just about anything as long as I know *God loves me this much!*

Hang on this week because we have some digging deeper to do. We have some very important roots that need to be planted and some extravagant, unimaginable love to experience!!!

5 LOVE LOSS

With the loss of those little lives locked in my heart and dealing with the loss of normalcy with Ashlyn, next God allowed me to walk through a season of loss of love.

I am going to share our "love story." Some of what I am going to share is excerpts from our book, "The30daysexchallenge-A Journey to Intimacy," a book that detailed our battle to save our marriage during this period of our lives. I republish it here as these events are an integral part of my story.

I know in the beginning of our relationship Paul and I had that kind of goofy grin some call the look of love. We all try to play it off like we don't act or look that way but, when it comes right down to it, true love does start out with that romantic ga-ga acting, emotional stage. In fact, my family caught me on video during that early ga-ga stage. It happened back in the early 90's when the handheld video camera was selling like hot cakes. I remember I was in our upstairs bathroom, brushing my teeth, and awaiting Paul's arrival. I had not seen him for a whopping whole week! He was driving all the way from Tampa to Indiana, an 18-hour drive, just to be with me over the holidays and to ask my father for my hand in marriage.

My brother-in-law had gotten the camera as a present from his parents for Christmas, and he was filming almost everything! As I was brushing my teeth, he came around the corner and asked if I was excited to see Paul. In a goofy voice, I replied, "He's the most wonderful man in the world!"

Paul and I had been great friends the previous spring semester and had taken a few drama classes together. He would flirt with me during class and then take his umbrella to pick up his girlfriend. I was pretty much over the initial attention he had given me by the time we hit our summer break. Still, I wrote him a friendly letter just to see how he was doing. He later told me he received a letter the same day from his girlfriend, but he found himself opening my letter first. Our friendship, and that's all it was at this point, continued when we went back to school in the fall. In the first few days of being back at college, Paul's girlfriend told him she had to leave for the semester to help at home with some family problems. He told me it was over between them. Their relationship had failed to deepen. In her absence, Paul realized whatever had been between them was over and it had been for a while. We didn't start dating right away. In fact, most of my friends thought that he was interested in my baby sister who had just started college as a freshman. It was my senior year, and I had always been serious about not dating unless I really felt the guy was a potential life-long mate. As a result, I really didn't date much at all in college. Now Paul, on the other hand, was what we term today as "a playa." Well, not really, but he was as much as one could be a "playa" in a little conservative Christian college. One night it was storming, as it does frequently in Chattanooga, and I didn't have an umbrella to walk to the dining hall. I called Paul up and asked him to come and walk me to dinner with his umbrella. This is the point in our story where Paul swears I was interested in him as more than just a good friend. But, since I am telling the story, I am sticking to my rendition, and I really just didn't want to get wet!

52

A few days later it seemed as if we were spending much of our free time together, and he finally asked me to go on an official date. Those early official dates were great because we were such great friends. It just seemed natural. I remember he took me to one of the many civil war parks in the area. As we were hiking, he took my hand. Now that was where the oddness struck. I actually was taken back a bit by the gesture. I knew our friendship was strong, but I hadn't yet viewed our relationship in true dating terms. I guess we started with a physical attraction for each other, one that has never been extinguished to this day. We got engaged that January and spent the next college semester apart. He moved home to save up some money, and I completed my four-year degree. We were married on May 19, 1990.

The first few years of our marriage were really fairy-tale in nature. With bits and pieces of it flawed with two selfish characters that were very self-centered and strong-willed. This combination didn't fly sometimes, and when life and our selfish desires interfered with God's plans and purposes for our lives, most of the time we took the easy way out and ignored our differences. We would move from conflict to peace without really resolving our self-centeredness and without really working on changing our relationship. We simply allowed life to happen, and we fell into what we now call "the drift." This drift lasted a while and would eventually trigger events that would change our lives forever.

Those who can recognize the drift are at a deep advantage. For most of us, it is called the drift because it is unrecognizable. I liken the drift to a current in the ocean, each wave gently pulling a raft rider out to sea. First, the rider drifts a mere three feet. No danger there. Then, the rider finds himself five feet. Still no cause for worry. Then, without warning, the rider finds his raft 30 feet down the shore. He looks up from a relaxing moment to a moment of panic. It's a sudden discovery of "I'm not where I once was." And then, puzzlement. "How did I get down here?"

I believe any relationship left to itself will experience a drift. Knowing what I know now, I realize Paul and I were not smart about our relationship. We simply felt so secure in our "bond of Christian marriage," we failed to recognize the current that began to tow us apart. We were drifting.

Despite the effects of the drift, life goes on. As our story goes, we became quite successful in our careers. On the outside things appeared grand. On the inside, things were not so rosy. We fought a lot. Always behind closed doors because everyone knows a youth pastor has to keep up appearances. We thought things are as good as they get! After all, no one is perfect, right? Sadly, even in church groups, we didn't talk about relationships too much. Plus, we were totally consumed with the busyness of our lives.

Five years into our marriage, Ashlyn finally arrived on March 3, 1999. She seemed different from other infants, fair skinned and unconcernedly border-line preemie weight. Her low weight didn't alarm the doctors, and we felt so blessed just to have our precious baby finally in our arms.

In those years immediately after Ashlyn's birth, our relationship was held together at best by a combination of companionship and faith. When you throw in a little "special needs" child… voila! Can you say train wreck? Our relationship spiraled down quickly during this time in our lives. We moved to another church ministry, in another part of the country, far from home. I was at home consumed with Ashlyn and Paul was working hard to grow another youth ministry. We both were going our separate ways, doing our own thing. I can see now there was definitely a lack of intimacy between us. Strangely enough, the problem was not a lack of sex. In fact, during this period we had gotten pregnant two more times! Sadly, those pregnancies ended in the loss of Baby November and Baby Spring. Back to back miscarriages.

I know I am starting to sound like Job! Seriously, it does get better but, unfortunately, not before it gets worse! There is always more to our hurts than meets the eye. In our case, the hurts just kept piling up. Now, I know my pain was not as severe as mothers who lose babies and are without hope. I firmly believe God is in control, and those babies are in Heaven. Still, experiencing the loss of those children and dealing with the challenges of a mentally handicapped child became utterly overwhelming! Life was exhausting, and we had little support at that time in our lives since we had moved away from family. This was especially true for Paul. He really missed a couple of close friends and his hometown. With all of these components in our lives running rampant, we both escaped from it all in our own ways. God seemed distant during this time. We kept saying and preaching the truth, but not living what we believed and expounded. Our marriage had degenerated dramatically.

At first, the distance became sort of familiar to me. As time passed, I noticed a detachment in Paul. I knew our relationship was different. I guess you could describe it as women's intuition or a gut feeling. There was nothing concrete, but I knew something was wrong.

As God always has it, He never lets His children continue in sin without making great effort to bring them back to Himself. One evening as Paul and I were driving home, I asked some probing questions and he began to reveal to me the truth about his distance. However short-lived, he had been having an affair with another woman.

He was very broken about it. It's what we call in church language, "repentant." He never left me. Not one moment did he leave me alone in those hours that followed his confession. Even when I would go into another room, Paul would come in and wipe away my tears and gently say with tears in his eyes, "I'm sorry. I never wanted to hurt you. Please forgive me." I know it was God's plan for him to experience all of the pain and tears his unfaithfulness had caused me. I forgave him for his unfaithfulness, and he would comfort me over and over and continue to tell me how sorry he was he had hurt me. Paul is a very tender-hearted man, and I am so thankful to God for that. I am certain his tenderness was in part from his love for our Lord and what he had done through this sin against Him as well. By the next weekend, we had gone to our pastor, confessed everything, and resigned from the church. Our church gave us the opportunity to say we were sorry before the entire congregation. Yes, "we" because as a couple I had to admit I had contributed to this immoral relationship by not meeting what we have come to understand as his "emotional needs" as a wife. Paul explained to me the enemy would play the movie just so far in his head, but the ending with all of the ugly consequences would never be revealed. So he would just see the great parts, the fun, but never the tragedy, pain, and loss of what his sin would ultimately cause.

As God had known, we already had a plan in place to leave for a week's vacation at home in Tampa. On the long drive home I ended up driving into the late hours of the night. Ashlyn was sleeping and Paul was resting as well. It was on that drive home I remember God speaking to my heart so clearly it was almost in an audible voice. I remember it verbatim to this day. He spoke gently and softly and posed the question, "Susie, if I can forgive him, then how can you do less?" I know I already said I had forgiven him, but as humans, something happens when we are hurt so deeply to the core of our very being. We have a very difficult time "forgetting" and so in those hours and days after the confession, I would think of questions and wanted to know all of the details. I would even awaken in the middle of the night for weeks upon weeks thinking about them together. I even had dreams he left us and I would wake up in a cold sweat, distraught and emotional. Again, he would comfort me and ask for forgiveness.

Still, in that drive home, I knew if Jesus could forgive him, forgive his hands, his feet, every part of his being, then how could I do less. You see from a young child I had been taught the Scripture that says, "Forgive as the Lord forgave you." (Colossians 3:13b)

You must make allowance for each other's faults and forgive the person who offends you. Remember, the Lord forgave you, so you must forgive others.

I knew Christ had forgiven me of much in my life. Who's to say, it could have been Paul as the victim and me as the unfaithful spouse? We all have it in us to be unfaithful. We are all just a step away from it. But by God's grace, it wasn't me. Still, I had to learn how to forgive, not just once, but often. And as I did, God healed my broken heart. As thoughts would race through my mind, I would quickly defuse them and whisper, "No, I have already forgiven that." I would then quote the Scripture again, "I forgive even as I have been forgiven." I learned to walk in that verse. It was hourly at first, then less frequently during the course of a day. Finally, there was a day I didn't even think about it at all! God is so good. I had always heard the phrase, "time heals all hurts." I believe now, God does heal all hurts.

As far as our ministry went, we had several people tell us we could no longer be in vocational ministry. After 18 months of working on our marriage, I just wasn't believing that my loving God was for that. However, I am not ignorant of the Scriptures in the Psalms that talk about the shame that follows anyone who is unfaithful and the far-reaching effects on his family forever. But the Scripture also says, I am the righteousness of God through Christ," which means we no longer have to live under condemnation or wear a scarlet letter. When God forgives us, He forgets our sins as "far as the east is from the west, He remembers our sin no more." When we are in Christ and forgiven by his blood, the blood HE so willingly gave on the cross, He makes us righteous before God. Not anything we do, but what He did. So, I held close to my heart the truths of those Scriptures.

Paul had been broken and repentant. I knew in my heart that counted significantly to God!

I am not making light of the severe consequences that go along with immorality and the far-reaching effects our sin had on the body of the little church and the youth in Virginia! It hurts my heart to think about it all to this day. Still, God has been very gracious in allowing us to see God work in some of those youth in spite of our failures as role models to them. You see, it never is about the man as much as it is about God. We fail, but God never fails! That is a huge lesson I have learned, and one we all should heed. We are human, and we fail. God is the only unfailing love. The only unfailing One! And what God has taught us over and over again is when God restores, He restores completely. What some people fail to understand is that God doesn't take our gifts and calling away when we fail. He is in the business of complete restoration.

This complete restoration was evident as we served at a great church in suburban Tampa. God did some incredible things and He used our time at that ministry to launch us into the unknown of church planting! In the summer of 2004, Paul and I and two other couples met in our living room to pray about what God would have Relevant Church to be.

Have you suffered a loss of love? How did you deal that loss?

Obviously, Paul's choice was not God's will for our lives. Still, God allows bad consequences to happen because we have a will of our own, and we make poor choices. So, where does God fit into your thinking about this idea that God gives us a free will and then allows us to suffer due to others' bad choices?

Maybe your loss is not a love loss but a hurt that runs deep, and you still have not recovered. Have you been able to forgive the hurt?

I know mine and Paul's greatest and most effective ministry has occured after our restoration. I have come to believe firmly that God uses broken people to reach broken people.

If you walk away from today's message with anything significant, I pray it would be the precept we are to forgive as Christ has forgiven us. I understand there may be things that happen to us that seem unforgivable. I believe as we try to model forgiveness the way Christ forgives us, we will only be better for it. Let's look at Colossians 3:13 once more.

In the New International Version, it says, "Bear with each other and forgive whatever grievances you may have against one another. Forgive as the Lord forgave you."

Do you see the phrase "whatever grievances you may have against one another?" I know many couples we have counseled have had what we call a "deal breaker" in their minds as they entered into marriage. Yet we see God's way doesn't make allowances for our "deal breakers." It says, whatever grievances.

The New Living Translation states it this way, "Make allowance for each other's faults and forgive anyone who offends you." So, we are not only to forgive whatever it is that offends us, but also we are to forgive anyone! You mean I have to forgive that nasty, noisy neighbor that is mean to my kids? Yes, I mean, anyone. And I have to forgive that teacher that has humiliated my child on more than one occasion during the school year? Yes, anyone. Do I have to forgive those who have not asked for forgiveness? Well, as hard as it may seem, if we are following Christ's model, He forgave all the sins of the entire world on the cross. Still, some have not received or accepted His forgiveness. Unfortunately, there may be those you offer forgiveness to who will reject your offer.

Reconciliation is the theme or message of the Bible. In the garden, Adam and Eve walked and talked with God in the cool of the evening. Their relationship was close, and nothing came between them. This is how God intended to dwell with His creation, with you and me. Still, had it not been for Eve's wrong choice there would have been no need for a sacrifice. Had it not been for sin, we would have Heaven on Earth. I believe God's heart is first for us to be reconciled to Himself through Jesus. Then, His heart is that we live in unity with others. This leads us to our key text in our Ephesians study.

Ephesians 4:2-3 (NIV) says, "Be completely humble and gentle; be patient, bearing with one another in love. Make every effort to keep the unity of the Spirit through the bond of peace."

I think when we extend forgiveness to those that have hurt us, even knowing in our heart of hearts they probably will just balk at our attempt, we have fulfilled what the verse means when it says, "making *every* effort...to keep the unity of the Spirit."

Notice the same word bearing is used in Colossians 3:13 (NASB). This word in the Greek means to sustain, to bear, and to endure. We are to endure offenses because unity is so important. But why is unity so vitally important in our relationships? The key reason relates to what John says about the unity of believers in John 17:23 (NIV), "I in them and you in me-so that they may be brought to complete unity. Then the world will know that you sent me and have loved them even as you have loved me."

Then the world will know when you and I forgive. When you and I are in unity, the world will know.

If our mandate is to make Jesus famous, to make Him known so those not yet in Christ will come to know Him, then it is vitally important we make every effort to keep unity.

Yes, we can choose to refuse to forgive. We can hold onto loss, hold on to our pain, even become bitter because of it. It is our choice after all.

But as for me, I choose to forgive. Before moving into your study today, let's take a few moments to consider the love losses you have incurred.

Questions For Reflection:

What love loss or losses have I incurred that have really affected my life?

Have I truly extended forgiveness to my offender?

In what ways have my response to the previous question influenced my life?

6 PLANS & PURPOSES

As I was contemplating the name of this study, one of the titles I considered was Grace. The reason I was considering Grace, other than the obvious, was that long titles didn't seem to be as marketable as a short one-word title. And, simply put, I liked it. As you know by now, I didn't pick Grace.

Still, I find it funny I picked the word grace to describe my story because my name, Susanna or Susan, actually means "full of grace." The meaning of my name didn't even dawn on me until I saw it in black ink on the written page. Believe me, I would never describe myself as "full of grace!" Graceful is just not an adjective I would use to describe myself. More like bumble, stumble, or even blunt, but full of grace? No.

The only reason I knew the meaning of my name is I received a bookmark in my tween years as a gift from my grandmother and it contained the definition. As I recall, this gift was sort of a big deal because my sisters didn't get one. I remember years later looking up the meaning of grace. I wondered if I embodied any attribute found in the definition of my name. I did not recognize anything graceful in me. Full of herself maybe, but not full of grace.

I kept that pink "Meaning of a Name" bookmark in my Bible for many years. I wonder to this day if my Godly grandmother prayed I would someday live up to my name? It is interesting to look back over what is probably half of my life now, and see the ebbs and flows that have transpired. To see how

God gifted me and has prepared me to be the person I am today and to fulfill the ministries He has called me to do.

As my interest was sparked concerning biblical names and their meanings, I found a blog in which a rabbi answered the question, "Why do I need to have a Hebrew name?" The most obvious reason to me was their use in religious practices such as a call to prayer. Most interesting to me was the idea the naming of a Jewish baby was called a "minor prophecy" of the parents. Some believe the child's name conforms to the inborn nature of their soul. Now, I am not asking anyone to do research on your name, but I am asking you to consider your life. Think about who you have become. Ask those who have had great influence on your life what they see in you - your character, your nature. What do they say about you? Who do they say you are? What is it that you do that has meaning and purpose?

After reading the intimate details of my life here in these pages, you should know parts of me pretty well. This is who I am and how God wired me. As you continue to study in Ephesians, we will discover God has wired you in a very special way, too. In fact, He has given us all gifts as His children. These gifts are for us to use and not just unto ourselves. In fact, the primary purpose of our gifts is rarely for ourselves but for the accomplishment of the works He has planned for us from long ago.

Do you understand how you are wired? Do you know your God-given gift? I believe my purpose is to use my gift of writing to help women understand just how much God really loves them. Now, I didn't come to fully understand my purpose until 40 years into my life! What I have learned over the years is in God's economy, our purposes and plans usually do not come into full bloom until we go through a process of refining, wrestling, and becoming.

Whether I like it or not, the description of grace embodies who I have become. The name was not chosen by me but given to me as though God knew what my life would be and that I would indeed fulfill my name. Of course, I believe God did know me and knows me now, that He is intricately involved in my life both personally and actively. He did know before time began I would be a person to live out loud the meaning of grace. Grace: to be merciful, to pardon. (Merriam-Webster)

I would have never dreamed I would have to pardon my husband for being unfaithful to me. It is astonishing to me the way God uses everything in our lives to teach us and make and mold us. I am not as merciful as I should be, but experiencing the grace of God in and through loss of love and then reconciliation of that love has made me more merciful. I guess in retrospect the name "Susan-full of grace" isn't as nerdy as I once thought. In fact, it is pretty cool God would choose to use me as He has. For that, I am very grateful.

God sometimes takes a lifetime to make us into what He wants us to be.

Take heart; there is a lot of Scripture that speaks directly to our purposes.

Let's start with Ephesians 5:10. "And find out what is pleasing to the Lord." Now, skip down to verses 15-17, "So be careful how you live, not as fools but as those who are wise. Make the most of every opportunity for doing good in these evil days. Don't act thoughtlessly, but try to understand what the Lord wants you **to do.**"

Our instruction today is rooted in finding the answers to these questions. What does the Lord want me to do? What is God's will for my life? What is my purpose?

One thing is for sure; the Bible clearly states we are not to be fools about it, not wasting time. We are to make the most of every opportunity. It is imperative and must be a priority for us as believers. We are not to be thoughtless about our lives, but we are to thoughtfully understand and think it through. We are to find out what it is we are to do. We are going to narrow in on the to do today because I believe God has something uniquely planned and specially designed for each of us.

God doesn't just leave us with a lingering question. In Ephesians 4 we have very specific direction in answering this question of "What does the Lord want me to do?"

Let's start back at Ephesians 4:4-16.

"[4]There is one body and one Spirit-- just as you were called to one hope when you were called-- [5]one Lord, one faith, one baptism; [6]one God and Father of all, who is over all and through all and in all. [7]But to each one of us grace has been given as Christ apportioned it. [8]This is why it says: "When he ascended on high, he led captives in his train and gave gifts to men." [9](What does "he ascended" mean except that he also descended to the lower, earthly regions? [10]He who descended is the very one who ascended higher than all the heavens, in order to fill the whole universe.) [11]It was he who gave some to be apostles, some to be prophets, some to be evangelists, and some to be pastors and teachers, [12] to prepare God's people for works of service, so that the body of Christ may be built up [13]until we all reach unity in the faith and in the knowledge of the Son of God and become mature, attaining to the whole measure of the fullness of Christ. [14]Then we will no longer be infants, tossed back and forth by the waves, and blown here and there by every wind of teaching and by the cunning and craftiness of men in their deceitful scheming. [15]Instead, speaking the truth in love, we will in all things grow up into him who is the Head, that is, Christ. [16]From him the whole body, joined and held together by every supporting ligament, grows and builds itself up in love, as each part does its work."

As we studied in chapters one and two, we learned who we are and whose we are. Here in verse 16 of Chapter 4, we see our work restated for emphasis. We see our purpose and plan is "to do" those works from Ephesians 2:10, "For we are God's workmanship, created in Christ Jesus to do good works, which God prepared in advance for us to do."

I pray you feel the heavy weight of the responsibility of our *to do* this day, and I pray you will really dig in deeply to know exactly what God is speaking to you to do.

God placed a passion within my heart and soul to get His message of love and peace to others. It began with music and blossomed. Singing came easily for me and I would find great satisfaction in ministering to people through music. Yet, as I grew up, I had a longing deep inside of me to teach, but I was not good at speaking. I felt like God forgot to give me a huge piece of my puzzle. I couldn't get words out of my mouth that made any sense. I honestly felt like Moses when God told him to go to Pharaoh, and he said, "But…I can't talk?" He complained so much that God sent Joshua to speak for him. I didn't want to be like Moses. What is so humorous is the fact I ended up teaching kindergarten. Kids are oh so much more forgiving than adults and they truly were interested in what I had to say. But I guess teaching kids is a speaking engagement with a captive audience. They are stuck with me whether they like me or not!

So here is what I want you to see and how I want you to connect the dots of your life with my story. God has a plan and purpose for our lives. He gives us passions to carry out our purposes. I thought my passion was music. Now I understand it was not just the music, but also the message God purposed for me to convey. He plants a passion in our hearts. We might more likely recognize it as a life goal or dream. Sometimes we recognize our passion or dream in what we call a "holy discontent," that thing we can't get away from that bothers us and we feel a need to make it right. It may be that thing that keeps us up at night. Whatever the case, we are passionate about that thing.

I don't have a clue what your thing may be. I could not tell you your passion if my life depended on it. I can tell you God has a plan and your purpose is to fulfill that dream. It is your calling. It is your **to do**!

Some of you are probably a bit puzzled right now because you were just like I was for 30 years. God, I have these gifts and dreams in my heart, but things just don't seem to be working out.

Let me speak a little more to God's economy:

We have dreams but with most dreams, there is a delay.

Take David for example.

He was anointed to be King as a boy. His daddy calls him out of the field to see the prophet. Next thing he knows the crazy man is pouring oil all over his head! As quickly as he was called to the house, I am certain he probably ran off into the field to shepherd his flock wondering what just happened. With his head dripping with oil, he might have asked himself, "Am I really going to be a king?" "When?" Think of how hard it would be to get that anointing oil out of your hair without modern shampoo! I don't know if David spent time wondering what it would be like to be King, but I do know he must have had doubts about his destiny. When Saul had David on the run for years, seeking to murder him, I am certain David had doubts.

Now take Joshua as another example.

God used Joshua to scout out the land of Canaan. Moses sent 12 spies to check out the land and report back so the people would be prepared to take the land as God had instructed them

68

to do. All but two came back and declared the mission would be "suicidal." Basically, they said, "God must be wrong, we CAN'T take the land. The people are giants!" But Caleb and Joshua said they could do it with God's help.

God planted a dream deep inside of Joshua. A dream to take the land! His dream was delayed 40 years. Because of the unbelief of the people, Joshua wandered along with the unbelieving generation. Don't you think he had doubts in those 40 years of wandering? But the story tells us Joshua stayed faithful. He didn't give up on his dream. God used the delay to develop Joshua so when he was ready, he was really ready! He called upon God to make the sun stand still, to lead the people through a raging river over to a little town called Jericho, where the "walls came a tumbling down!" (KJV, Joshua 5 & 6)

Now let's look at Joseph.

Joseph was the dreamer. God literally gave him a dream showing him his brothers would bow down to him one day. That didn't set right with his older brothers.

His dream was delayed when his loving brothers tossed him into a pit. He was falsely accused by his boss's wife, then imprisoned. Yet, in the delay, he developed! I am sure he was certainly discouraged at times and experienced doubt about "just what are you doing with me, God?"

Anyone been there?

I know exactly what some of you are thinking. For some of you, your lives are so messed up you can't see how God could use you. Others of you are thinking, I have no clue as to my God-given passion and purpose! Some of you may even be thinking the only to dos on my to do list are laundry, dishes, and more laundry! I understand, believe me. Still, one thing I don't want you to miss in all of this is found in Ephesians 4:16. "From him the whole body, joined and held together by every supporting ligament, grows and builds itself up in love, as each part does its work."

You are part of a whole; you have your own special work. But the greatest news here is: "He makes the whole body fit together *perfectly!*" It is His work that accomplishes the work. "He who began a good work in you will be faithful to complete it in you." (Philippians 1:6 KJV)

He gives you your dream, but there is almost always a delay filled with doubt and development so you can know and be ready in His perfect timing to accomplish the plans and purposes of your **to do**!

God has a plan. Are you in on His plan? He has given you a passion. He is preparing you for your **to do**, for your God-given purpose!

John 3:27 says, "a man can receive only what is given him from heaven." (NIV) Has God given you a dream? Maybe you find yourself in the delay part of your dream. If you are in that "waiting place," as Dr. Seuss describes this part of life, remember God is using this time for your development to your full destiny! Yeah, now I'm starting to preach it like T. D. Jakes, but it is truth!

I heard it once said, "the days are long and the years are short." We have very little time on this earth. Scripture says, "Your life is like a vapor that appears for a short time then vanishes away." (James 4:14)

Questions For Reflection:
As you look back at your life thus far, maybe your name has a meaning that is totally opposite of who you are. Maybe you are grateful you are not living up to the meaning of your name. Yet, if you were to describe yourself in a few brief words, what would you say about yourself? Even more important is this question: What do others say about you?

70

In this little time we get to call our life, what is your greatest longing or desire? Have you narrowed your search to find how God has gifted you? What are you passionate about? Do you know your purpose?

Are you reaching for those plans God has prepared for you before you were even a twinkle in your daddy's eye?

*If not, what are some steps you can take to thoughtfully consider your **to do**?*

As we study this week in Ephesians 5, take the time to consider verse 17 and find out what pleases the Lord, or "what the will of the Lord is."

God has a plan. He has given you a passion. He is preparing you. He's developing you for your purpose!!! He is preparing you for your **to do**!

As always, dear one, remember God has chosen you. You are His. You are a princess. You have an inheritance because…

God loves you this much!!!

7 RELATIONSHIPS

If you will permit me to stay in Chapter 5 of Ephesians for a bit longer, I need to completely unpack what God has on my heart about our relationships. I must admit I have not been overly excited about this message for two reasons. One, I am lacking in my very practice of these biblical truths that I am giving to you. And secondly, these biblical truths tend to be a bit controversial in Christianity today.

These truths are controversial in the very nature they are used in marriage ceremonies, and controversial in how they have been preached from the pulpit. These are difficult passages to grasp for several reasons. We will take a look at some of those reasons later in the chapter. First, I want us to take a step back and look at the entire picture of these biblical truth, like an artist steps back from his painting to see the entire picture in this way, we can take in the vastness of what God is trying to get through to our sometimes hard heads and ultimately, our hearts. Would you be willing to set aside all of your presuppositions and be opened minded enough to truly hear a word from God that might just oppose the very core of who you are and what you have been told your entire life?

You see, as girls we are products of the *girl power* generation. We are influenced by our culture whether we believe it to be biblical or not! We may not know what that the cultures of our past stood for or what they accomplished, yet we are products of that generation simply because our mothers lived through an era that embraced woman's rights. Unfortunately, instead of Bible-believing women taking a stand for what is right and honorable, some of the women leading the charge taught against the Bible. I believe some biblical principles got confused and trampled upon during the past 75 years.

I am not slamming our equality, our advancement in society, or even a cultural movement. I don't even want to go there! Even writing this today, all I want to do is make jokes about being *strong, independent women!"*

> *'Cause I can bring home the bacon*
> *Na na na na!!!*
> *Fry it up in a pan.*
> *and never let you forget you're a man,*
> *cause I'M a WOMAN! W.O.M.A.N!*

We all applaud our gender and clap for our accomplishments. Yet. as funny as that all is, what if we have fallen prey to a plan that has its root way back in the garden? What if we are carrying over the effects of Eve's choice and Adam's silence? What if we are fulfilling the curse on womanhood and preventing the God-breathed purpose, plan and position for our gender, woman, female, you and I? Let me make clear that this conversation is completely about marital, biblical roles in our homes. God does not speak against women and their roles outside of the home. He is a God of equality.

I want to consider several passages that are seen as archaic and controversial, even in our church today. With open minds and hearts, let us listen to the words of God as directed specifically at us, a collaboration of the truths of Scripture for our female gender:

"[9]But the LORD God called to the man, "Where are you?"

[10]He answered, "I heard you in the garden, and I was afraid because I was naked; so I hid."

[11]And he said, "Who told you that you were naked? Have you eaten from the tree that I commanded you not to eat from?"

[12]The man said, "The woman you put here with me-- she gave me some fruit from the tree, and I ate it."

[13]Then the LORD God said to the woman, "What is this you have done?" The woman said, "The serpent deceived me, and I ate."

[14]So the LORD God said to the serpent, "Because you have done this, "Cursed are you above all the livestock and all the wild animals! You will crawl on your belly and you will eat dust all the days of your life.

[15]And I will put enmity between you and the woman, and between your offspring and hers; he will crush your head, and you will strike his heel."

[16]To the woman he said, "I will greatly increase your pains in childbearing; with pain you will give birth to children. Your desire will be for your husband, and he will rule over you."

[17]To Adam he said, "Because you listened to your wife and ate from the tree about which I commanded you, 'You must not eat of it,' "Cursed is the ground because of you; through painful toil you will eat of it all the days of your life.

[18]It will produce thorns and thistles for you, and you will eat the plants of the field.

[19]By the sweat of your brow you will eat your food until you return to the ground, since from it you were taken; for dust you are and to dust you will return." (Genesis 3:9-19)

It is pretty straight forward stuff here. They both chose to sin, blamed others, and needed a God given attitude adjustment in the form of consequences to the human race.

Unfortunately, the consequences, or curses as they are called in many Bible translations, are carried down from generation to generation. We are cursed because we were born female and men are cursed because they were born male. The passage means, "through painful toil" the man will work hard for his living. Whatever they end up with as a career, it is work, work, and more work, to make a living with all the weight that responsibility making a living carries. The minute each male child is born into this world he is cursed because of Adam's curse.

Let's look a little closer at our female curses because they do affect us whether we want to acknowledge them or not.

The first curse for the female is easy to decipher. We have pain in child-birth. Even with modern medicine, and praise the Lord for those medicines, we still have pain.

The second curse is the one that often gets mistranslated. I believe part of this stems from the fact that most preachers are male, and most men think much differently than we think. In my experience, I have only heard this second curse taught in the context of sexual desire, that wives will desire our mates or want our men sexually. I have always found this interpretation odd, as it seems to me, most of the time, in sexual relations, it is the man desiring the woman! Simply put, and as a blow to many a male's ego, the *desire to control* doesn't have anything to do with sexual intimacy.

What then does the "desire" imply? The curse is that our desire will be to rule over our husbands. This is not a sexual desire, as some have taught before, and we can't blame men, as every man wants to believe their woman *desires* them! But no, this curse means that we desire to *rise up* and rule over our men!

76

Thus, the battle between the sexes began way back in the garden and continues to this day

With this as our foundational biblical truth today, it's our blasted curse, and our strong desire to rise up and control or be in control, let's look at our very controversial Ephesians passage for our study today.

"[21]Submit to one another out of reverence for Christ. [22]Wives, submit yourselves to your own husbands as you do to the Lord. [23]For the husband is the head of the wife as Christ is the head of the church, his body, of which he is the Savior. [24]Now as the church submits to Christ, so also wives should submit to their husbands in everything. [25]Husbands, love your wives, just as Christ loved the church and gave himself up for her [26]to make her holy, cleansing her by the washing with water through the word, [27]and to present her to himself as a radiant church, without stain or wrinkle or any other blemish, but holy and blameless. [28]In this same way, husbands ought to love their wives as their own bodies. He who loves his wife loves himself. [29]After all, no one ever hated their own body, but they feed and care for their body, just as Christ does the church— [30]for we are members of his body. [31]"For this reason a man will leave his father and mother and be united to his wife, and the two will become one flesh." [32]This is a profound mystery—but I am talking about Christ and the church. 33However, each one of you also must love his wife as he loves himself, and the wife must respect her husband." (Ephesians 5:21-33)

So here we see a little *love* and *respect* in action, yet it seems to me that many Christian relationships struggle with these biblical truths more than we are willing to admit. But how in the world do we get to a peaceful and happy balance of love and respect? And in keeping with our study, how do the curses or consequences of Genesis speak to this love and respect?

Let us look at the key verse 22, "Wives, submit yourselves to your own husbands as you do to the Lord"

Bingo! No wonder we are instructed to come under our husband's authority. It is our curse after all! Right? And what a curse it is!

I admit, I struggle with wanting to rise up and take control of things in my house right in front of my kids a lot of times. It is a blasted curse. Anyone know what I mean? I don't really want to be in charge. He is fully capable, but I do it anyway! And it comes oh so comfortably to me!

Can you relate? I believe this desire for control is out of control in our homes! As women, we have been taught to aspire, strive, and sacrifice a lot to reach certain position or status in this world's economy. I believe this is a result of our enemy's plan to confuse and set our marital relationships up to fail. If we can rule in the business world, then we should rule in our homes right? This false thinking has crept into our thinking and even our biblical theology.

But what if this is all wrong? And what if we are not to be in control, not to rise up? What if we are already, the minute we are born, born into a God-given position, even one of honor? May I submit to you to consider as we strive with all our might, determined even more than ever to gain new ground for ourselves, what if we are, in reality, losing ground? What if we are replacing the God-given position, which I believe is one of honor, love, protection and peace, with a false sense of position? A position that we are not wired to manage, hold, or carry the weight from in our homes. A key question to ask yourself is, "Do I believe the curse is punishment or correction?" If we think about the consequences of Genesis as only punishment for the human race, both male and female, I believe we drastically miss out on the grace of God that is evident throughout all of Scripture. Yes, the curses are curses. And yes, the initial sin of both Adam and Eve eating the apple of disobedience caused the separation from God that is only ultimately restored through the shed blood of Jesus on the cross. Still, the grace of God is experienced in every couple that loves and respects in the order of the truths of Scripture.

I am not saying that women are weak. That is the first lie of the enemy. We are not to be doormats, nor are we to be underestimated. God placed woman in spiritual authority back in Judges. When men did not take on their roles properly, God used women. I am not saying that women cannot lead outside of their marriages either. Many women are more effective as leaders than men in many aspects of our culture. These ideologies are simply more lies from our enemy. Proverbs 31 is evidence of a strong, successful, businesswoman.

Let's take a glimpse at this Godly wonder woman.

> [10]A wife of noble character who can find?
>> She is worth far more than rubies.
> [11]Her husband has full confidence in her
>> and lacks nothing of value.
> [12]She brings him good, not harm,
>> all the days of her life.
> [13]She selects wool and flax
>> and works with eager hands.
> [14]She is like the merchant ships,
>> bringing her food from afar.
> [15]She gets up while it is still night;
>> she provides food for her family
>> and portions for her female servants.
> [16]She considers a field and buys it;
>> out of her earnings she plants a vineyard.

¹⁷She sets about her work vigorously;
>   her arms are strong for her tasks.
¹⁸She sees that her trading is profitable,
>   and her lamp does not go out at night.
¹⁹In her hand she holds the distaff
>   and grasps the spindle with her fingers.
²⁰She opens her arms to the poor
>   and extends her hands to the needy.
²¹When it snows, she has no fear for her household;
>   for all of them are clothed in scarlet.
²²She makes coverings for her bed;
>   she is clothed in fine linen and purple.
²³Her husband is respected at the city gate,
>   where he takes his seat among the elders of the
>   land.
²⁴She makes linen garments and sells them,
>   and supplies the merchants with sashes.
²⁵She is clothed with strength and dignity;
>   she can laugh at the days to come.
²⁶She speaks with wisdom,
>   and faithful instruction is on her tongue.
²⁷She watches over the affairs of her household
>   and does not eat the bread of idleness.
²⁸Her children arise and call her blessed;
>   her husband also, and he praises her:
²⁹"Many women do noble things,
>   but you surpass them all." (Proverbs 31:10-29)

This woman is not a quiet, living in the shadows of her husband kind of woman. In fact, she is out there doing her business like nobody's business. Her man is respected in the streets in front of all of the men of the town, and her kids and hubby rise up and "call her blessed!" What I want everyone to get is this. Her family is a priority. She is loved and cherished! She also has protection, peace, security, and soundness of mind; this woman is living in her God-given position. She has it all! In God's economy, Christ is the head, our husbands are the heads of our homes, and we are to "submit to (our husbands) as unto the Lord!"

He is the head. We are the heart. We are already in a place of honor, Girls. Do you see it? This is the grace factor of God that is given in and through the consequences or curses of Genesis!

So how do we fulfill this foreign concept of *submission* that we see in Ephesians 5 and which we quite frankly and honestly despise? How do we submit? How does love and respect work?

The how is in the root of what the Bible teaches us about love. You see we cannot take only a few Scriptures about the marital relationship and expect to fully understand our roles. We need to study and digest as much as possible to come into a full understanding of our relationships. We need to learn the specifics of our roles. We need to know the why behind the role. Why would God ask the female to submit? Does he prefer male over female? These questions are imperative to weigh.

We can better understand why we are instructed to submit because our curse tells us that we naturally will **not** want to submit! We desire to rise up and rule over our husbands. These instructions make a lot more sense in context of understanding our curse.

No, God doesn't like men more than women! Get it through your head now. I know we will not be able to hit every verse in the entire Bible concerning this hot button issue, but we need to start the conversation and dig into it. After all, it is our role!

Since loving each other is our ultimate goal here, let's examine a few verses on love and their meanings.

God's love obviously is sacrificial, and Jesus is our model. We know that love is not founded in the "feelings" of love. Any sustainable relationship is built upon true love, which is a noun. We know that love is a choice to stick it out when the going gets tough. Enduring love is also sacrificial as seen in the Greek word, **agape**. Agape love is Jesus' unconditional, sacrificial love for us, a love that expects nothing in return.

Another biblical word for love that we should understand is the Old Testament word for God's love, **haceed**. This word haceed is found in many Old Testament passages of Scripture, and its meaning is primarily based upon a reciprocal, covenant love. There is a passage in Hosea in which the haceed word for love represents relationship.

"I want you to show love, not offer sacrifices." (Hosea 6:6)

"Haceed is representative of our English interpretation in most of these verses as God's faithful love. This love is true. It conveys the idea of covenant as in the marital relationship and in which both parties (spouses) are loyal and owe to one another this *faithful* love. That is why it is used to mean the covenant love or faithful love of God the Father to the children of Israel. The difference for us today is to understand the New Covenant where Jesus conveys the word love as agape. Agape expresses not only unconditional, sacrificial love, but also the idea that this love is given with nothing expected in return.

Did you catch that last phrase?

Nothing is expected in return! As we agape our spouses, we model Jesus' love for us. He died for us expecting nothing in return. These expressions of the word love, both covenant haceed in the Old Testament and the New Testament Greek word agape, must be grasped as we discuss the love relationships that God desires for us as His children.

Interestingly, if you were to look up the meaning of the word haceed, in the common Hebrew language of today, you would find this definition: "An overwhelming desire to give yourself to the other person for their benefit regardless of the cost to you.".[5]

Please hang with me another minute to see this next connection. There is an amazing similarity to this meaning of haceed in God's faithful love to us as seen in the passage in 1 Corinthians 7 that uses our English word **please** with regard to how we are to treat our spouse and in return how they are to please us. This word please is aresko in the Greek, which means to accommodate oneself to the desires, opinions, and interests of others.[6] Notice the almost identical mandate in both of these words, the word aresko, please, as compared to the word haceed, love. This idea of giving yourself to the other person, putting their needs before your own, is represented in Scripture in both words. And these words are paramount to understanding the instruction to marriage partners on the subject of *how* they are to engage one another. This is God's plan as to how we are to love each other, how we are able to love and respect each other.

If we are to gain nothing else from this lesson on relationships, let it be an understanding of this one fact, marital love is sacrificial. It is putting the other person before yourself. If we can understand this, then we will have gained valuable wisdom for our relationships. If we but put into practice this idea alone, what a difference it could make in our marriages.

I stand here with no evidence or intent to try to tell you that I practice this haceed love all of the time. Nor do I aresko, please, my husband like I should. I am certainly a far cry from an example of agape love, I tell you!!!! Yet I am not ignorant of the fact that this is biblical truth, is either taken, shaken down and rooted deep within us or it can be like water off a duck's back.

So, now what? What do we do when truth is presented to us, especially truth that is controversial, shocking, and even a paradigm shift in our thinking?

If you are still with me and I didn't lose you over the whole submitting idea, then you may be asking the question: What then does our role, the female honor position, look like in practical daily events and circumstances, and in modern marriages?

Glad you asked! Here is what it looks like for me. As you know, I usually start the lesson with my story and end up with God's story intertwined, and, hopefully, your story makes some connection along the way. Today I end with my story.

Believe me, I am still a work in progress. This so goes against my natural inclinations, instincts, habits, and personality that I am almost sick just writing this message to you this hour! You see, I am a teacher and I like to rule my classroom. I really struggle with being in control. My father even once said of our family at a reunion dinner, "The problem with this family has always been, too many chiefs and not enough Indians!"

But here it goes.

As long as I have been married, I have been in the shadows of my blessed husband. In our early years, I pushed hubby through college, supported his educational aspirations for nine years, and I put my dreams, my goals and my desires on hold.

Sound uncannily familiar to the definition of a particular verse?

Well, as I put into practice our Greek word "aresko,"I accommodated myself to his dreams, opinions, and desires. But, what was I getting in return? I got a big bag of infidelity in return. But did I quit? No. I choose to love. I grabbed a good dose of haceed, covenant love, and held on to it tightly, as did he!

84

To make a long story short, now I am known for what every woman in America wants to be known for: "The sex pastor's wife!" Maybe that is what I should have titled my book!!!

Without even knowing it, I was practicing what I would now be preaching: simple acts of preferring his success, pushing him to the front of the limelight, stuffing my dreams aside…Okay, pause a moment…

If any of you truly know me, you know that I rarely stuff too much aside, and I still make my opinion known. But it sounds so much better for me to look like the martyr here, however, I know you all see right through me.

Now there have been times I have not done what I know Paul wants me to do, and there have been times I have not done what he has told me to do right away. Truth be told, there were times when I was that quarrelsome woman in the house, nag, nag, nagging. (Proverbs 25:24) Still, I can honestly say that over the last 27 years of marriage, I can rarely remember a time that I went against what he said to do.

If we are to love as God loves, give sacrificially as Jesus gives, then what is this expectation of *submission* and *our honorable position* in our relationships all about?

Unbeknownst to me, the times that I submitted must have outweighed the times that I revolted or tried to rise up because, in God' economy, I am sitting pretty in a place of honor. Not one of my making, but one of my husband's making. I am a *kept woman* as he likes to put it! I am a cherished woman. As he is esteemed in public, as he is known and as he makes Jesus famous in the city, so am I known. In fact, there is a sense that overcomes you as you see God use your husband in a very miraculous way. It is like the feeling that comes over you the first time your child gets the citizenship award over all those other kids in the class! It is like he has gotten the "Best Servant Award for Making Jesus Famous!"

I am proud of him! And I am reminded of what James 4:6 says, "God resists the proud, but gives grace to the humble." Each time as we humble ourselves to our head, God first, then our spouse as our head, we are receiving grace because of our humility and our obedience. Think of the position of honor once again because later in James 4, verse 10 states "Humble yourselves before the Lord, and He will lift you up in honor." (NIV 1984)

This is God's way. This is His economy. As we obey, He lifts us up on to that position of honor. All I can encourage you to do today is listen to him! Do what he says, even when you don't want to, and even when you think he is wrong.

I really despise the idea of submitting to him! But when I really think about it, I shouldn't despise my God-given role. I should despise the curse! So, there you have it...like it or not.

I am preaching to myself you know. We are born to rebel. We do not like doing what others tell us to do. We would prefer just doing it on our own, on our own time table, and in accordance with our own will. Still, life is made of choices. We can live peaceably in our God-given position, or venture off and ultimately out from under the protection of our husbands, out on our own.

The times I have chosen to venture out from under the protection of that loving umbrella called my head, my husband, out on my own, I must admit those are the times I have been burned!

In the garden, the roles of male and female were perfect. They were a perfect fit, so to speak. We were made to complete man. We were intended to fill the void of loneliness and help our mates. Not vice versa. But for that blasted curse!!!

God made another way for us to be loved and cherished. He gives us this position of honor, a place of protection, peace, and security. They carry the weight of providing for the family, and loving us as Christ loved the church. We are simply to respect.

As we lean into our intended purpose as a completer, helper, recipient of love, adorned and cherished above all other creations, living in our God-given position, even with all of our natural inclinations in opposition to this submission thing; and against all that culture tells us and even going against all that our mammas have worked to instill in us, we are woman. When we follow God's economy, we not only get to experience the grace of God in our curse, we get to enjoy the relationship of love, intimacy, and companionship that was God's original plan. I believe we even make the curse of Genesis easier for our husbands to carry.

Then and only then do we walk out God's economy, God's intended relationship as seen in the garden. We are born to be honored. We are born to be cherished and loved by our husbands! And that is man's role, and another whole Bible study! As we live in our God-given roles, submitting to one another as seen in our study passage, and then submitting to our husbands as unto Christ, we bring God's intended plan for marriage back to earth. We get to experience a glimpse of what garden life was like, and what the hope of eternity with Christ will be like. Still, most importantly, we show a lost world that we trust in God as our Maker and Creator. We tell the world that we believe in God's plan and purpose for our marriage relationships over our culture and over our curse!

Questions for reflection:
How would you compare your marriage with the love and respect marriage of the Bible?

What bothers you about being under the head of your husband?

Think about all of the ways the Proverbs 31 woman puts her family first.

Can you think of any adjustments that you can make to love your husband without expecting love in return?

This week I parked at the end of Ephesians 5. This was intentional because I felt the need to emphasize our marital relationships. If we are not strong in our marriages, we lose our effectiveness to the world. In fact, chapter 6 of Ephesians could almost be connected to chapter 5 in that our relationship theme carries into much of the first several verses of chapter 6. As we continue to study Ephesians this week, I pray our relationships grow and mirror Christ's love for the church. Be diligent, dear one and remember...*God loves you this much!*

8 PEACE PRINCIPLE

Today's lesson begins with excerpts from what morphed into a segment of journal entries during the most fearful and conflicting time of my entire life so far. When I tried to re-write the experiences, I decided to leave some of it as journal entries because it seemed to me the rawness of the daily emotional and spiritual battles would be more helpful to someone going through what I went through.

As I sat down to finally try to complete this book. I admit it has been yet another year since I have written much. I always start with reading and rereading, thinking and praying of how God would have the message of this book to be laid out. Little did I know that the following 72 hours would change me forever.

Journal Entry #1

Last week, our "prince" as we like to refer to him, our son, Anthony who is now 11 years old going on 18, was complaining about his left forearm hurting. I waited several days to finally take him to a walk-in clinic near us, thinking he may have a simple fracture since it continued to be painful and now looked a little swollen. The doctor x-rayed the arm and found a suspicious and very peculiar looking cyst or something, in his left radius bone. Not something this doctor had seen evidently, because he looked at me like a dear in headlights, which is always a comforting expression to realize on your physician's face. When I asked what it could be in the bone, he just said, "I don't know." Grrrreat! He doesn't know!! Now comforting words to go along with his bugged-out eyes! The nurse was very gracious and asked if I wanted her to make an appointment for that afternoon to see an orthopedic physician in town. Sure. I remarked. I was eager to find out what had invaded my baby boys arm and get it extracted and healed as quickly as possible. Three hours later we found ourselves in the orthopedics' office and he tried his best not to make us nervous when he ordered, a bone scan, CT scan, MRI and blood work for the following day, just to rule out anything like a tumor!

As one could imagine our stomachs sank at even the thought that our son could have a terrible bone cancer. We set up the tests, twittered for prayer, and went against the doctor's advice to put on Facebook that our son could have a tumor. As people of faith, we needed prayer! As I have come to realize over the past several days, the effectual, fervent prayer does avail much! In the following hours, it took so much out of me emotionally and physically, just to call our immediate family and try to explain what had just happened in the last few hours. I never have had more bombardment of evil thoughts then what I experienced in those short, few hours after first hearing the possible bad news! I remember driving home from that day of office visits feeling kind of stunned. Thinking how could we be here? This was just supposed to be an arm fracture at worst. I shouldn't be even considering the thought that my baby boy could have some life-threatening cancer.

Journal Entry #2

I couldn't sleep much last night; I tossed and turned and finally woke up around 4am.

The Lord brought to my mind the Psalms

'Yeah tho I walk thru the shadow of the valley of death, I will fear no evil. Thy rod and Thy staff they comfort me."

It has been a very long time since I have felt the gravity of death in my personal world.

And I have never contemplated the fact that the even the "shadow" of the valley of death has enough fear in and of itself alone. The idea that our prince could be snatched away from us by a progressive bone cancer was the possibility, or "the shadow of death" for me. If nothing else, I pray that this experience, will be a reminder to me to comfort those who are going through tests. Before this experience, I would have said, "We are not going to worry about this situation until we get the test results back." Since my spiritual gift is not mercy, I never realized the impact of what I was saying. I was indeed saying, I don't believe you should be concerned about your life or the life of a loved one until there is need to be concerned. This is for shame on me, I see it now and I admit now that my practical approach gave little comfort to those in the "waiting room" of medical tests.

Journal Entry #3

Another amazing wonder that I am experiencing through this trial is the power of the prayers of believers. While my faith is stronger, it has been those prayers that have literally kept my mind affixed to the only source of strength that we have, Jesus.

Evil is always captured or allowed to roam freely in our thoughts and hearts by our willful choices. What I mean is when we think a negative producing thought, whether planted in our minds by ourselves or the evil one, we have a choice to make, right then and there. At that moment, we must capture the thought and bring it into subjection to align with Christ Jesus, or we will by default allow that evil thought to plant itself. We may even allow it to sprout roots, prosper and grow. That evil seed of thought may even take root so that it produces other fruit! This fruit will not be good fruit, but toxic, and destructive. This poisonous fruit may not only paralyze us but also choke the life out of us.

We have all experienced this happening in our minds if we just stop and analyze our thinking processes. An example is when I first heard the possibility that my son's arm had something growing in his bone, my mind went immediately to the fact that my grandfather had died of bone cancer. Next, that thought gave way to the thought that I know a man who is an amputee because his arm had bone cancer as a college student. The initial evil thought gave way to a myriad of destructive thoughts.

These thoughts do not only affect our minds, but they also affect our emotions. My calm, collective nervous system was torpedoed into nervous shock while my stomach plunged into my gut. So from thought to emotion, to literal sick feeling all within a matter of 5 minutes!

I am not saying that this is wrong, necessarily, this is the way God has wired our bodies to handle the major stresses of life. Still, when we allow these negative seeds of thought to rule and reign in our minds, take root and start budding, then we are going against what I believe is the peace principle.

What about your life? Have you had the "phone call" that drove you straight to your knees in prayer? Have you experienced that ugly sickening feeling that comes from bad news? In life, we all face these moments and how we cope with them in the moment will depend upon how we are grounded now. Let's talk about the peace principle in our study time today.

The peace principle comes from many Scriptures.

Thou wilt keep him in perfect peace whose mind is stayed on Thee because he trusteth in Thee. (Isaiah 26:3)

When we practice the peace principle we are saying no to our minds, wills, and emotions, and saying, yes to Jesus. We oppose our thoughts and we trust in Jesus. We contradict the world's view and trust Jesus view. We align our thinking with the mind of Christ. It is the will of Christ that we would be more like Him and have the mind of Christ.

This peace principle is not a one-shot deal. It is not a silver bullet to an "all is well here" mind set.

Journal Entry #3 Continued
The hours and days to follow were some of the toughest that I have ever endured. The fact that there was a very real possibility that his cyst may not biopsy benign is still a possibility today as I write.

Amazingly the prayers of our friends and family continue to carry me in these last few hours before the actual biopsy and procedure. Yet the principle of peace is still present."

Journal Entry # 4
Six days into the news, God has helped my heart and mind in His gentle way. He used music, at times, Christian television broadcasts, twitters and Facebook messages at just the perfect time. Each of these moments I recognize now as the Holy Spirit's sweet whispers to confirm His presence and the "peace principle" at work in my life.

During this time I remember turning on the radio and hearing the words "praise You in the storm", not the entire song, but the prevalent message. "Ok, Lord, I don't feel like praising you in this storm, because quite frankly, I don't want to go through this storm," I stated emphatically to Him riding along in my minivan! I have had enough storms to endure, and You want me to praise You in this storm? Yes, I questioned my faith in that fact. And at church that next Sunday, our worship team sang the David Crowder Band song "He loves you". Oh, I sang under my breath, trying to process the idea that I don't think that I would ever really believe that God loves me, if Anthony has cancer. Honestly, this trial was the hardest of my entire life. Harder than miscarriages, harder than almost losing my husband to an affair, harder than losing our ministry for a time, and harder than the daily loss of raising a mentally retarded child! Not that I love Anthony more than anyone else, I think it is the fact that he has been our joy in the midst of storms! He is our Solomon, our gift in the midst of sin. He is our blessing from the fruits of repentance, our future and hope. He seemed to be the untouchable one. And now I must realize that he is not mine. He is not untouchable. None of us are. I remember thinking, "I will not give him over to the enemy, nor am I ready to release him over completely for God to do with what He wills for good. And I don't see good in cancer!"

That night I woke up at 4am and couldn't get back to sleep. I remember thinking about the verse that the Word of God is sharper than a two-edged sword, cutting to even the marrow and the bone. I thought that the Sprit wanted us to pray the truth of the Word of God into his little radial bone. I recall asking the Lord, "What truth?" The truth that I recalled the Spirit immediately gave to me was this verse, "He was wounded for our transgressions, He was bruised for our iniquities, surely He bore our sorrows, and by His stripes we are healed." (Isaiah 53:5) Even our sorrows were part of Christ's Jesus weight that he bore upon the cross. I never realized the magnitude of that truth. I had been taught that Christ's stripes heal our infirmities, yet being raised in a conservative church environment I really had not seen much supernatural healing. If I carry sorrow that He already bore on the cross for me, what a travesty! He bore not only our sin, but also our sorrow. I went back to sleep in peace that night with those wonderful truths of the Scripture as my sleeping pill.

I remember the morning of the tests. Each Christian personality that was on cable that morning spoke on faith, and healing. Coincidence? I firmly believe, that the Spirit was reminding me what I know to be truth so that I would not be consumed with the evil thoughts running rampant in my mind. The main verse that ran across the screen was James 5:15, "The prayer offered in faith will make the sick person well." (NIV) I began to speak that truth and try to keep my heart wrapped around the prayer of faith.

It was now one week from discovery, and three days before scheduled surgery. Ashlyn had caught the flu, and I became preoccupied with getting her well and keeping everyone else well. The prayers of believers carried me through this unknown daily journey and peace was prevailing.

This book became my daily retreat from the reality of life and the next entry that I wrote was this

Journal Entry #5
The next time I write, I will have good news that the biopsy is benign, in faith, we pray and believe, and this chapter will be wrapped up as a week of spiritual testing...Sifting! A week that I do not ever want to revisit!

Journal Entry #6
Today is six days removed from his forearm surgery; the surgery went as we expected, accept there was a small micro-fracture so he is placed in a cast instead of a splint. And while the doctor still believes the cyst is not a cancerous tumor, the pathologists did not sign off until they took a week to run more tests! Ugh...is my initial reaction in my heart. Another week to wait!! I wanted this over with and now! But as I have learned over the years, most things are out of my control. Thankfully, God has continued to keep our minds sane while we wait the confirmation that the cyst is not cancerous. I believe in my heart that God heals, and I am believing God is right in the middle of

this waiting game, we call, a storm of life. Still, I find that I have to remind my mind to keep focused on peace, I must "keep my mind stayed upon Thee." It is working and aside from a few minor, mind slips, God has kept me in a peaceful state. However, I did call the doctor's office to ask if the test results were back yet. I got an answering machine.

Journal Entry #7
21 days into this walk thru the valley of the shadow of death, and I still find it amazing how that the prayers of God's people with my consistently speaking God's truth... "Thou wilt keep him in perfect peace whose mind is stayed on Thee because he trusts in Thee..." emphasis again on "because I trust in Thee and I know Thee very well!" is keeping me sane. Another great precept of God's Word is found in the function of the Holy Spirit. He is my comfort and my reminder. As I need the Truth, the Spirit reminds me of all Truth. Well, that which I have committed to memory or heard often. I am also comforted by the words of songs or even hymns that I sung as a child. One particularly stands out to me today, as I ponder in whom I am trusting and believing. "I know whom I have believed and am persuaded that He is able to keep that which I've committed unto Him against that day!" Funny that a couple of days ago the Lord blew our socks off by giving us some really beautiful home furnishings for such a great bargain. I know it came directly from His hand of blessing. Not that material means is something I normally hold as that important, but It was such a remarkable deal that it drew me to thankfulness knowing that God can work in any situation and circumstance if He so desires. He can make a new bone in Anthony and transform his being in an instant if God so desires to do it! Yet, when I called the doctor, today this little blessing became a little comfort as we realized that the pathologists were

96

now sending his diagnostic images for the national oncologists to view and that he was not in the clear yet! More waiting!

We will have troubles in this world according to the Scripture. So how do we prepare ourselves? Today's Scripture is an incredible lesson waiting to be learned if we take heart and apply it to our lives today.

We need to daily be ready for whatever our enemy, the devil throws at us. His plan for our lives is for our total demise! Our enemy desires to sift us like wheat

[31]"Simon, Simon, Satan has asked to sift each of you like wheat. [32]But I have prayed for you, Simon, that your faith may not fail. So when you have turned back, strengthen your brothers." (Luke 22:31-32)

Satan wants us to stumble, fall, sin, and give up when battles come our way Did you notice that we have more prayer coverage than just those in our family of faith? This passage states that even Jesus pleaded in prayer for Simon and that shows we can be confident that He is definitely for us as well!

Satan may have lost our souls to Jesus for eternity, but while we are still faithful witnesses here on earth, he wants to not only ruin the word of our testimony, but also ruin our lives!

So, just how do we protect against the enemy and how do we cling to the Peace Principle in our lives when siftings come our way and when the storms of life knock us to our knees?

Today's key text is our Ephesians passage that we dissected in the last few days of our study last week and our answer is to put on the whole armor of God.

Let's look at our key Scripture once again today.

"[10]Finally, be strong in the Lord and in his mighty power. [11]Put on the full armor of God so that you can take your stand against the devil's schemes. [12]For our struggle is not against flesh and blood, but against the rulers, against the authorities, against the powers of this dark world and against the spiritual forces of evil in the heavenly realms. [13]Therefore put on the full armor of God, so that when the day of evil comes, you may be able to stand your ground, and after you have done everything, to stand. [14]Stand firm then, with the belt of truth buckled around your waist, with the breastplate of righteousness in place, [15]and with your feet fitted with the readiness that comes from the gospel of peace. [16]In addition to all this, take up the shield of faith, with which you can extinguish all the flaming arrows of the evil one. [17]Take the helmet of salvation and the sword of the Spirit, which is the word of God. [18]And pray in the Spirit on all occasions with all kinds of prayers and requests. With this in mind, be alert and always keep on praying for all the saints." (Ephesians 6:10-18)

We are in a fierce battle, dear ones, a battle for our lives and our families. We need to know the truth and strap that truth on. We need to put on our faith, our helmet of Salvation. We need to know our faith is grounded in Jesus. We are His and He is our Father. We need to be ready to move at the beckoning call of our savior to share the truth of the Gospel which the Bible calls, "The Good News that is within us." We are to be ready with the Armor of God, not self-reliance or independence, but only of God and relying only in God, our strength. Remember, He is our peace and has broken down every wall. Our battle is not against flesh and blood, but it is a spiritual battle! And finally, we are to pray in the spirit at all times! Persistent in prayers and alert! Then we will stand firm against all the strategies of the devil.

So, what about the "prince?" I don't want to leave you hanging about our son's oncologist report.

Journal Entry #8

About two months from the day of our discovery of the blasted cyst, we received the news that even the National Oncologists now believe Anthony's cyst to be benign. Yes, to finally be able to announce this good news is a huge relief!

And now the doctor stated at his last x-ray, that he believed the cyst would never grow back or be a problem in Anthony's life. HALLELUIAH!!!

So why take you along this seemingly morbid downer of a journey?

Satan's plan was to sift us like wheat in this trial with our son Anthony! Our adversary, the devil, wanted us to stumble and fall into depression, if not to give up on God altogether. Whatever we would give him, that devil would take. Had it been fierce failure of faith, anger toward God, or even fear itself, he would laugh in our stumbling! But God, in His love and through the wonderful inheritance of faith that we have, we were able to withstand against the devil by putting on the armor of God. Still, as graciously as I can say this, don't think that you will be able to stand against the battle of the enemy if you are not in God's boot-camp daily. I am so thankful for Scripture memorized as a child and in adulthood. Time spent in God's Word and in His presence in praise is never wasted. It is the process of preparing for battle, the process of being ready for the wars of life to come, putting on the armor is vitally important in our spiritual journeys.

My prayer in taking you along with me in my journal is not that you will say, "Wow, Susie really held it together!" Although I was writing and journaling what was going on in my head and heart. There were times of utter fear and complete desperation! My prayer is that you will see that the Spirit of God does comfort us in times of trouble, and you will know the power of the prayers of Godly people in your life, and that you will grasp the importance of being ready for whatever life throws at you. As He comforted me, He will certainly do it for you if you are prayed up, armored up and alert to what is really going on in the spiritual realm of your life. Remember, we wrestle not against flesh and blood, but against spiritual enemies! In remembering, you will stand firm!

Questions For Reflection:
According to Isaiah 26:3, explain the "peace principle."

What makes keeping our mind, will, and emotions focused completely on Jesus so difficult?

Have you ever had a time when you believed the enemy was trying to "sift you like wheat?"

Have you ever had to practice the peace principle? How did you work through it?

I want to encourage you to do something special in addition to our homework. We began this study with my question "Does God really love me this much?" And as we conclude with the answer to that nagging question, I would like for you to take some time to think through all that we have learned together from our study of the book of Ephesians and to answer that question for yourself in the form of a love letter that you write from God to you. But I really want it to be more of an edict. What is an edict, one may ask? An edict is a decree, order, command, or mandate, a proclamation. I want this love letter to be filled with all truths from Scripture of how much God really loves you. I want you to decree this love letter to yourself and in times of trouble I want you to keep it accessible so that you can

100

command your mind, will, and emotions to keep focused on the one source that gives us comforting peace through the trials of our lives, Jesus. Finally, I want you to know most of all, that whatever battle you are facing today, *God loves you this much*! He really does!!!

A Final Word

Upon completing the rough draft of my story, a copy of a wonderful book was given to me at a time that I really needed a spiritual shot in the arm. And oh, I must not forget another character trait of God, as He is always timely.

This book is Kay Warren's book, wife of Pastor Rick Warren of Saddleback Church, "Joy - because happiness is not enough". I am sure you understand why the book was just what I needed to read at the time with the theme being joy. While the book was an incredible reminder to me, I decided to spend some time just thinking about the joy factor in my life. I had to admit that my misconception of joy has long plagued me to the point that I had given up on ever really living a joy filled life. Still, as I considered the words in her book, I came up with a summation of my own. Joy, not a personality type but the root that grows from a heart confident in God working all things together for my good, with praise as the fruit!

I had to stop and resonate with that redefined knowledge. I do have joy. No, I am not jovial all the time or even all smiles. Honestly, I am a cup-half-full sort of girl. But joy? Yeah, I'm not happy all the time, but I am confident that God is working all things together for my good. And when I rest in that assurance, the fruit on my lips is praise. That is how we can praise Him in the storms of life.

This new joy definition is like seeing life as a canvas of splattering, emotional events, some are good and some are bad and quite frankly, some are really bad. Yet, how we respond and in Whom we trust will determine our final portrait. Trust in self, a life utterly alone. Trust in others, a heart often left full of hurt. Still, trust in God that we can have hearts full of joy even in the storms.

Whether I knew it or not, this belief has been another core to sustaining peace and ultimately joy in all of my disappointing moments and all of my painful experiences in my life. This joy is also that which has kept me grounded when things were flying high and out of control in great ways. Even when I forget to trust in God, I am almost always directed back to the solid truths of Scripture.

I want to share a final journal entry from my personal devotional time for this final word.

Final Journal Entry #9
I realize now that I stumbled over a passage of Scripture a week ago, but today as I glanced over what I had digested earlier in the week, the passage became alive in a way that I can only give credit to God as the amazing author and praise to the Spirit for grabbing my attention. It is found in Lamentations. Yes, Lamentations a book of lamenting...seems appropriate.

"[19]my affliction and my wandering, the bitterness and the gall.

[20]I well remember them, and my soul is downcast within me.

[21]Yet this I call to mind and therefore I have hope:

[22]Because of the LORD's great love we are not consumed, for his compassions never fail.

[23]They are new every morning; great is your faithfulness.

[24]I say to myself, "The LORD is my portion; therefore I will wait for him."

[25]The LORD is good to those whose hope is in him, to the one who seeks him; Lamentations 3:19-25)

I decided all those months ago now that this would be my final exaltation and Scripture message.

It is so much of a summation of our journey together and my reflections with God through this journey that I want to share again some excerpts from the Message version with you. As we digest this wonderful Word, compare how the book of Ephesians mirrors so many of the same truths from the Old Testament book of Lamentations.

[19-21]"I'll never forget the trouble, the utter lostness,
the taste of ashes, the poison I've swallowed.
I remember it all – oh, how well I remember –
The feeling of hitting the bottom.
But there's one other thing I remember
And remembering, I keep a grip on hope:
[22-24]God's loyal love couldn't have run out,
his merciful love couldn't have dried up.
They're created new every morning.
How great your faithfulness!
I'm sticking with God. (I say it over and over).
He's all I've got left."
(The Message, Excerpts from Lamentations 3:19-25)

I'm sticking with God!

So, this is my edict, my proclamation for my life right now. Like the author of Lamentations, I will patiently wait for the salvation of the Lord. Maybe not as patiently as the prophet, but I will try to be patient as I journey with my companion, Jesus.

It seems like my life is full of grief and sorrow as I re-read over the pages of this book with you. Yet, I must exclaim to each reader that I do not feel it is so! My life thus far has been an adventure to say the least! I have been cared for, nurtured, encouraged, and cherished as a daughter. I have known and know a love that grows with each passing day that is given by a man who truly is my gift from God! He so cares and cherishes me! I have known the love of two children in ways that many cannot ever imagine and experienced the love of family that is greater than many will ever know. I know the most wondrous love of God as my Father, my Savior and most of all, my Companion. I can say that I have known the comfort that only the Spirit of God can bring. Life is better than good. Life is great! I have been a part of daily miracles and experienced modern miracles on a daily basis. I've been blessed to experience first-hand God grow a church from six to six hundred in a matter of six years! I have seen God repair and restore our ministry from brokenness to wholeness to fruitfulness! I have the leisure to be who God created me to be. I get to exercise my gifting in various ways that others can only dream about. Yes, it is an understatement to say, God is good to me.

I'm sticking with HIM...GREAT IS HIS FAITHFULNESS TO ME! I know now and I proclaim, decree and mandate my edict... GOD LOVES ME THIS MUCH!

Acknowledgments

This work would not have been possible without the emotional and prayer support of my family and close friends. I am especially indebted to Lee Sullivan, for her extensive professional guidance and tireless hours to formatting both books. She has been supportive of my writing, and a huge encouragement in completing these books.

Notes

1. "God Makes No Mistakes" lyrics by by Kim Moore. © Copyright 1991
2. "Proorizo" Blue Letter Bible. "Dictionary and Word Search for proorizo (Strong's G4309)." Blue Letter Bible. 1996-2015. May 9, 2015
3. Complete Commentary on the Whole Bible, by Matthew Henry
4. Chan, Franes, *Crazy Love*. David C. Cook Publishers, 2008.
5. "Haceed" Blue Letter Bible. "Dictionary and Word Search for haceed (Strong's)." Blue Letter Bible. 1996-2015. May 25th, 2015
6. Blue Letter Bible. "Dictionary and Word Search for aresko (Strong's G700)." Blue Letter Bible. 1996-2015. April 20, 2015

Made in the USA
Columbia, SC
23 August 2017